Cocktails at Pam's

&

Evelyn Strange

a mystery

two plays by Stewart Lemoine

Playwrights Canada Press
Toronto • Canada

Cocktails at Pam's © Copyright 1985, 1991 Stewart Lemoine
Evelyn Strange © Copyright 1995 Stewart Lemoine
Playwrights Canada Press
54 Wolseley St., 2nd Floor, Toronto, Ontario, Canada M5T 1A5
tel: (416) 703-0201 fax: (416) 703-0059
e-mail: cdplays@interlog.com   http://www.puc.ca

Playwrights Canada Press publishes with the generous assistance of
The Canada Council for the Arts – Writing and Publishing Section
and the Ontario Arts Council.

Playwright photo by Jeff Haslam.

CANADIAN CATALOGUING IN PUBLICATION DATA

Lemoine, Stewart
        Cocktails at Pam's and Evelyn Strange
A play
ISBN 0-88754-539-4
I. Title. II. Title: Cocktails at Pam's and Evelyn Strange
PS8573.E552C62 1997   C812'.54 C97-931397-X
PR9199.3.L44C62 1997

First edition: January 1998.
Printed and bound in Winnipeg, Manitoba, Canada.

For Louis and Margaret Lemoine

Stewart Lemoine lives in Edmonton, Alberta, where he's
been writing and directing for Teatro La Quindicina since the
first Fringe Festival in 1982. He is the author of more than
thirty full-length and one-act plays, several of which have
been seen across Canada in Teatro productions. These include
the Dora Mavor Moore Award-winning "The Vile Governess
and Other Psychodramas", as well as "Shockers Delight!",
"The Glittering Heart", "When Girls Collide", and "What
Gives / All Ears". Among his more recent works are "Connie
in Egypt", "The Book of Tobit", "The Velvet Shock", "The
Lake of the Heart", and "Pith!"; and the young audience
plays "The Hothouse Prince", "The Spanish Abbess of
Pilsen", and "The Subject of My Affections". Stewart is a
three-time winner of Edmonton's Elizabeth Sterling Haynes
Award for Outstanding New Play.

Playwright's Foreword

I'm not sure why, but my first impulse in writing a Foreword for these plays is to attempt to find some profound and significant connections between the two. On further reflection, this seems potentially taxing, so I'm not going to bother. Cocktails are downed in both works and quips are fired off at regular intervals, but beyond that... I'll leave this subject for the academics. It might be a little more pertinent for me to describe the experience of writing these two plays, since the processes were quite different.

I wrote "Cocktails at Pam's" in 1985, about two or three years after I'd taken to writing seriously, and having things produced. The success of my early works was encouraging, but it also created a tiny incipient panic in me about my ability to create on demand. I do believe that when writing is your job, you must forego the impulse to be emotional or precious about it, so I set out to cure myself by resolving to write every day for at least a month, whether I felt inspired or not, and the result was the play you now have before you.

After creating a number of small oddball playlets, I hit upon the idea of writing a cocktail party. Since a social event of this sort has its own predictable schedule (arrival of guests, first round of drinks, more guests, more drinks, canapés, etc.), the challenge of structuring the play was not the least bit daunting, and I was able to concentrate on making up characters and having them talk and talk and talk. Odd as it may seem, writing scenes for large groups of people always comes a little more easily to me, and I suppose that's just because someone's always able to offer a new point of view or just change the subject completely.

As the play progressed, it became clearer and clearer to me just how high the stakes could be for Pam Cochrane at her party and, as I'm an opera fan, a big mad scene seemed utterly in order. To those who would scout the first part of the play looking for some clue as to why Pam goes insane by way of Scotland, I offer the following advice: Oh stop. No one wrote better madwomen than Sir Walter Scott and Pam's brogue is a tribute to his Lucy – *The Bride of Lammermoor* – and my own favourite, Madge Wildfire in *The Heart of Mid-Lothian*. And as long as I'm confessing to arbitrariness, I should also say that Estelle's green-pepper tirade was a previously existing diatribe exercise, for which I merely created a context. Since this monologue's inclusion in *The Perfect Piece: Monologues from Canadian Plays* (Playwrights Canada Press) in 1991, it's become such a staple of the audition circuit that it now seems to be the one piece of my writing for which I'm most likely to be remembered. It's a good thing then, that it comes from the heart.

Writing "Evelyn Strange" a decade later was a very different experience. I'm not about to hold forth on "plotting mystery fiction", but creating a work of this sort does present certain very particular challenges for a playwright and the greatest of these is writing plausible dialogue. The play's success depends so much on information being deliberately withheld and then deliberately revealed, and this must be accomplished within the limits of conversational discourse. Making up the "what happened" part isn't so difficult, but revealing that through the interaction of four characters, each with a completely different set of secrets and suspicions... now that's tricky. I'd say it's the most technically challenging thing I've attempted, and there were days when, like Evelyn, I thought so hard I could almost feel my brain move. The best way to cope – long walks. I've also found that sitting and pondering always leads too quickly to napping, so when faced with a seemingly hopeless tangle of plot points, I must move through space. Like Perry Spangler, I would appreciate that forward motion leads to clear thinking. I'd also say that it's the only part of the playwriting process with clearly discernible cardiovascular benefits.

Of further reflection, I'd say there's one very important point of contact between these two plays, and indeed all the others I've written. This lies in the degree to which they reflect the fantastic diversity and interpretive scope and humour and panache of the actors of Teatro La Quindicina. It has been my great good fortune to have these individuals in my life to inspire me to write these plays and then to bring them so successfully to the stage. I would pay particular tribute on this occasion to Leona Brausen, Jane Spidell, Davina Stewart, Julien Arnold, Jeff Haslam, and John Kirkpatrick, and to thank them for convincing me that I actually know what I'm doing.

Stewart Lemoine
September 1997

"Cocktails at Pam's" was first produced by Teatro La Quindicina at the Edmonton Fringe Festival in August of 1986. The cast was as follows:

PAM	*Davina Stewart*
JULIUS	*Jeff Bredt*
RITA	*Kathleen Bednar*
CYNTHIA	*Jane Spidell*
LEON	*Phil Zyp*
SARA	*Leona Brausen*
VIRGIL	*Gary Lloyd*
MAX	*Warren Sulatycky*
DENISE	*Cathleen Rootsaert*
LILY	*Darcia Parada*
ESTELLE	*Marianne Copithorne*

Directed by Stewart Lemoine.

The current edition was revised for Teatro La Quindicina's revival at the 1991 Edmonton Fringe Festival.

PAM	*Davina Stewart*
JULIUS	*Jeff Haslam*
RITA	*Bridget Ryan*
CYNTHIA	*Jane Spidell*
LEON	*John Kirkpatrick*
SARA	*Leona Brausen*
VIRGIL	*Frank Manfredi*
MAX	*Julien Arnold*
DENISE	*Cathleen Rootsaert*
LILY	*Andrea House*
ESTELLE	*Barbara Gates Wilson*

Directed by Stewart Lemoine
Designed by Roger Shultz

It is strongly recommended that the word hostess be read with the accent on the second syllable.

Cocktails at Pam's

The elegant living room of PAM and JULIUS COCHRANE. It is late on a summer afternoon in 1965, PAM enters wearing a beautiful cocktail dress. She perches on one of her tasteful chairs and looks about the room.

PAM (*sighing*) Ah, lovely. Lovely chair. You, lovely room...

JULIUS enters, knotting his tie.

JULIUS Pam, you're talking and there's no one here.

PAM Ah ha ha. I was just making some comments to the living room.

JULIUS Oh?

PAM I was remarking on how beautiful everything is right now, and I don't simply mean the exquisite furnishings, superbly lit and accented with only the most nonpareil of objets d'art, There's a special glow here, as though the room itself were anticipating another wonderful cocktail party. I know, I know, technically a furnished room cannot have feelings but...

She walks expansively amongst the furniture.

I have put so much of myself in here. Each vase, each end table, each little throw rug is a part of me, It seems only fitting that I share my emotions with the living room.

JULIUS Might as well.

PAM Oh Julius, I hope our little soiree will be a success. Just think of it darling. People drinking, talking to one another...

JULIUS No doubt about it. We'll have a regular riot of fun.

PAM Now Julius, don't get carried away. Something can always go wrong,

JULIUS It can but it won't. Everything will be fine. After all Pam, you've never failed anything in your life,

PAM (*smiling radiantly*) That's true. (*turning abruptly*) Well now, I must go and give Rita her pep talk before the guests begin to arrive. Do you know where she is?

JULIUS I expect she's in the kitchen where she belongs,

PAM Julius, Rita is the maid. The maid doesn't belong in the kitchen. The cook does. If we had a cook, that's where she'd be.

JULIUS Where does the maid belong then? In the living room? The dining room?

PAM Oh no. No, no. The dining room is for guests. The living room is for householders, or on this occasion for guests as well. I'd say there is no one proper place for a maid. She must be in constant motion.

JULIUS Like a shark?

PAM Like a hostess.

JULIUS Well if you're going to be in constant motion, I hope none of the guests mistake you for the maid.

PAM Not likely, since I'll be in pearls and a gown, (*laughing rather suddenly*) Oh my. Such banter! Such repartee! At this rate, I'll be exhausted in five minutes.

JULIUS Oh-oh.

PAM Exactly.

She laughs again and exits quickly. JULIUS puts on his jacket and goes to the bar. He pours himself a drink and begins to set out some glasses and bottles, whistling a popular tune of the day. The doorbell chimes.

JULIUS   (*to himself*) The door.

RITA crosses hurriedly.

There's no need to sprint, Rita. No one's that eager to get in here,

RITA   I'm sorry, Mr. Cochrane.

JULIUS   You might trip and whack your head. I've done that.

RITA goes off and reenters almost immediately.

RITA   Miss Dallas is here.

JULIUS   I don't know her. Is she a beauty contestant?

RITA   Maybe.

JULIUS   I didn't think Pam knew any of those. Well ... show her in.

RITA steps out and returns with CYNTHIA DALLAS, an attractive and stylishly dressed young woman.

JULIUS   Ahh ... So you're Miss Dallas. What a pleasure to meet you. My name is Julius Cochrane, I'm married to the hostess.

CYNTHIA   (*shaking his hand*) How do you do?

JULIUS   I must confess I've never visited your part of the world, but I fully intend to one day. It's the calf-roping that appeals to me, I don't know why. Have you ever roped a calf?

CYNTHIA   No. No, I haven't.

JULIUS	Really? Hmmm. Well I suppose oil keeps you busy. I think people tend to forget that Texans have moved into the twentieth century. You must have an opinion about that, as their representative
CYNTHIA	I ...uh ... I'm not certain ...
JULIUS	Do you know anything about the oil industry?
CYNTHIA	Not really. I'm an actress.
JULIUS	You are?
CYNTHIA	Yes.
JULIUS	Well well. I guess there's nothing too strange about that. It just proves one shouldn't have any preconceptions about you Lone Star State folks.
CYNTHIA	I don't know what you're talking about. I'm from New York City.
JULIUS	But ... How did you get to be Miss Dallas?
CYNTHIA	What? Oh ... Dallas is my name. I'm Cynthia Dallas.
JULIUS	(*laughing*) Oh of course, of course. You must get that all the time.
CYNTHIA	Actually no. This is the first time it's ever come up.
JULIUS	Really?
CYNTHIA	Yes, but it is kind of funny when you think about it. Miss Dallas.

She laughs. JULIUS laughs also. PAM enters.

PAM	Mirth! Mirth!

JULIUS and CYNTHIA turn and look at PAM.

PAM	Cynthia. Here you are! You've met my husband Julius.

CYNTHIA   Yes.

PAM   Cynthia is an actress.

JULIUS   Yes, I know.

PAM   She's from New York City.

JULIUS   I know that too.

PAM   (*to CYNTHIA*) How long have you been here?

CYNTHIA   About two minutes.

PAM   That long? Well if you'll excuse me, I must go back to the kitchen. Julius, did you know that Cynthia is appearing in *King Lear* at Stratford?

JULIUS   No, I had no idea.

PAM   (*exiting*) Well well, now we've got the ball rolling.

JULIUS   *King Lear*? Hmmm, I'm not sure I've seen that one. We went to something at Stratford last month, but I don't recall what it was. We had very good seats. Actually we go to Stratford fairly often because it's just close. But then you know that don't you? How is it you know my wife?

CYNTHIA   Last week the ladies auxiliary gave a luncheon for the cast. I was seated next to Pam.

JULIUS   Is that a fact? That's how I met her too. We were seated next to one another in a restaurant. Though not at the same table. Will you have a drink?

CYNTHIA   Oh yes, please.

JULIUS   What would you like?

CYNTHIA   Oh ... a Gin Fizz. Can you make those?

JULIUS   Absolutely, yes. (*going behind the bar*) So, I take it you aren't acting this evening.

CYNTHIA   Oh no. It's Monday. We never act on Mondays.

JULIUS   That's interesting. Actually that's strange. Is it a religious thing? Do you have to do laundry? What ...

CYNTHIA   I don't know. It wasn't my idea, I suppose it's so we get a regular day off and people can still go to the theatre on weekends.

JULIUS   Ah, sensible. And who wants to go to the theatre on Monday anyway? Or ever.

CYNTHIA   Well, I...uhhh...

JULIUS   Oh, I'm sorry, I just meant ... whenever I go to the theatre it's not because I want to, it's because Pam has bought tickets. I suppose if it were left long enough, I might discover that I did want to go, but so far I haven't had the chance to find out because she always beats me to it.

CYNTHIA   Oh, that's too bad. I'll bet it just drives you crazy.

JULIUS   Not really. You see, I manage an airline and my mind is usually occupied with that.

CYNTHIA   Oh, is that what you do? Pam just said that you were in business.

JULIUS   I think that's all she knows. It's what I told her when we first met, and the subject hasn't come up since. Though I have changed jobs on at least two occasions.

The doorbell chimes.

JULIUS   (*to himself*) The door ...

RITA   (*walking through the room at a stately pace*) I'll get it.

JULIUS   Rita has never been a maid before.

CYNTHIA   Oh my.

Before RITA crosses the room, LEON bounds in.

LEON	Greetings!!
RITA	Eeee! Mr. Bandelier has arrived!
	She turns and flees.
LEON	(*carrying flowers and a sketch pad*) I let myself in. I hope you won't tell Pam.
JULIUS	Too late. Rita's probably telling her now,
LEON	Oh-oh.
JULIUS	It wouldn't hurt you to wait until Rita answers the door.
LEON	I suppose not. I know it's important to Pam, but I am her brother.
JULIUS	And Rita is her maid. Pam doesn't play favourites you know. Everyone has their function to perform. Say Leon, I'd like you to meet Miss Dallas. Miss Dallas, Mr. Bandelier.
CYNTHIA	I'm pleased to meet you.
LEON	Hey, you're Cynthia Dallas, the famous actress.
CYNTHIA	I'm not.
LEON	You are too. You're playing Cordelia at Stratford.
CYNTHIA	I meant I'm not famous.
JULIUS	I had no idea who she was.
LEON	You don't count Julius. You know nothing of the theatre.
JULIUS	Exactly, so I'm the best judge. If I'd recognized her, she'd have to be famous. Or someone I'd met before.
LEON	Well you're widely admired Miss Dallas, I can assure you of that.

CYNTHIA	Thank you very much.
LEON	Why, I'd give you these flowers, but I brought them for Pam.
CYNTHIA	It's quite alright.
PAM	(*entering*) Leon! Hello!
LEON	Pam! Hiya!
PAM	(*covering her face with one hand*) Hiya ... ?
LEON	Hello.
PAM	That's better. (*looking at her hand*) Oh, there's something on my hand. It's black, (*touching her face*) Oh (*quietly*) Julius, do I have something black on my nose?
JULIUS	(*winking*) No.
PAM	Oh ...

> *For the remainder of the scene, PAM believes that there is a black smudge on her nose, though this is not so.*

LEON	(*holding out flowers*) I brought you some flowers, Pam.
PAM	(*taking them tentatively*) Really? But I've already assembled a number of appropriate floral arrangements. There are no more suitable vases. (*handing the flowers back to LEON*) I'm sorry but I can't accept these.
LEON	What should I do with them?
PAM	You could offer them to Miss Dallas. You have met Miss Dallas haven't you?
LEON	As a matter of fact, I have. Only moments ago.
CYNTHIA	Please, everyone, call me Cynthia.

LEON	Would you like these flowers, Cynthia?
CYNTHIA	Oh. Thank you.
PAM	Well done, Leon.
CYNTHIA	(*opening the package*) Chrysanthemums! How lovely!
PAM	You didn't tell me they were chrysanthemums.
CYNTHIA	Would you like them back?
PAM	Oh ... of course not.
LEON	Say Pam, is there going to be food at this party?
PAM	What a question!
LEON	Well, this is the time of day when I usually eat dinner.
PAM	There will be little nibbles.
LEON	Hooray.
PAM	But not until more people arrive. Julius, no one has a drink but you.
JULIUS	Oh, I'm sorry, Cynthia, here's your cocktail.
CYNTHIA	Oh. Thank you.
LEON	Have you got one for me?
JULIUS	Not yet. What would you like?
LEON	A Gimlet.
JULIUS	A Gimlet? Let me see if I can remember...
LEON	It's like a Martini, only with a pearl onion rather than an olive.
PAM	That sounds like a good idea, since I don't care for olives, I had one in '59. Cynthia, what an experience!

JULIUS   Leon, I'm not sure that's what a Gimlet actually is.

CYNTHIA   I've heard of the drink you described, but I think it was called a Gibson.

PAM   A Gibson? Ah ha ha ha! That is the name of a person, not a cocktail!

> *She leaves the room, laughing musically.*

JULIUS   How about I make it and not worry about what it's called?

LEON   I want a Gimlet!

JULIUS   Do you care what's in it?

LEON   Not really, no.

JULIUS   (*picking up bottles*) Then I don't think we have a problem.

CYNTHIA   I wonder what I ought to do with these flowers?

LEON   Put them in a vase. (*he laughs*)

CYNTHIA   But Pam says there are no vases.

JULIUS   Don't worry about it.

> *JULIUS rings a hand bell, RITA leaps into the room.*

RITA   Hello.

JULIUS   Oh hello Rita, Miss Dallas has some flowers. Could you put them in some water, in a jar or a bucket and put them out of sight.

RITA   (*tentatively*) Well, I suppose...

JULIUS   Don't let Mrs. Cochrane see you, I think maybe the tool shed would be the best place for them.

CYNTHIA   I could put them in my car.

JULIUS   Oh, there's no need for that. Here Rita, quick, quick!

RITA   (*taking the flowers*) Oh, chrysanthemums. (*whispering to CYNTHIA*) You're lucky.

CYNTHIA   Thank you.

> *RITA scurries away.*

JULIUS   What's that pad you have there, Leon?

LEON   It's a sketchbook, I was out and about in the countryside today. I did all these sketches. See...

JULIUS   Let's have a look, (*sitting down with the book*) Oh. Birds. Trees. Oh. Flowers. Hmm ... These aren't very good, are they?

LEON   No, of course not, I can't draw,

JULIUS   Then why bother?

LEON   Because it's relaxing and peaceful and I enjoy it.

JULIUS   That's a bit perverse when you consider the results.

LEON   Maybe it's just that I'm so very bad at it, so hopeless, that there's no onus to improve. I think that's what I like.

JULIUS   (*giving back the book*) Well don't ever show me any of these again.

LEON   I don't think I'm liable to want to. (*to CYNTHIA*) Would you like to look at these?

CYNTHIA   Oh yes, thank you.

> *She flips through the pages.*

JULIUS   (*going to the bar*) Oh, Leon, here's your ... Gimlet.

LEON   Great, thanks. (*to CYNTHIA*) Well?

CYNTHIA	(giggling) Well ...
LEON	Hmmph!
CYNTHIA	Actually, I like this one of the tree here.
LEON	Ah yes, that line is quite straight isn't it.

The doorbell chimes.

JULIUS	The door ...

RITA runs through the room.

LEON	Go, Rita.
JULIUS	I wonder who it will be?
LEON	Does it matter?
JULIUS	I should think so. What if it's someone none of us knows?
LEON	They're bound to know Cynthia.
CYNTHIA	Ohhh.
RITA	(*entering*) The Blacks are here.
JULIUS	The Blacks?

Everyone looks faintly puzzled.

Oh, the Blacks! I know them.

LEON	I do too.
CYNTHIA	Well I don't, I've never met them.
VOICE	(*offstage*) Look Sara, it's Cynthia Dallas! *VIRGIL and SARA BLACK enter. They're rather imposing and a little intense.*
SARA	Oh yes. So it is. Hello. Hello, Julius. Hello Leon.

JULIUS	Hello.
LEON	Hiya. Hello.
VIRGIL	(*flatly*) Miss Dallas. It's a surprise and a pleasure to see you here.
CYNTHIA	Have we met somewhere before?
VIRGIL	Never. I'm Virgil Black and this is my wife Sara.

SARA smiles, briefly.

CYNTHIA	I'm pleased to meet you. Call me Cynthia.
VIRGIL	Well Cynthia, we were fortunate enough to see you in *King Lear* last week. We really enjoyed it.
CYNTHIA	Thank you very much.
VIRGIL	We were quite surprised. It's not often one actually enjoys *King Lear*.
CYNTHIA	Oh I know what you mean. It's so sad.
VIRGIL	But when you think about it, all the unpleasantness and killing are really important things for us to witness, since life can be sad and the world can be unpleasant and people are always being killed.
CYNTHIA	Don't I know it. I'm from New York City.
SARA	Are you sad, Cynthia? Is your life unpleasant?
CYNTHIA	Well, no ...
SARA	Has anyone ever tried to kill you?
CYNTHIA	Of course not. What a question. I ...
SARA	Julius, I'd like a scotch and soda.
JULIUS	Of course, Virgil, anything for you?

VIRGIL	I'll have a Gin Fizz.
CYNTHIA	That's what I'm having.
VIRGIL	Oh? Would you like me to have something else?
CYNTHIA	No, I...
SARA	Where's Pam?
LEON	She's around.
JULIUS	I think she's tending to things in the kitchen.
SARA	Oh, then there's going to be food?
JULIUS	Yes.
SARA	Good. We're missing dinner for this.
JULIUS	That's nice. Pam will be pleased.
	PAM enters.
PAM	Ow! Did someone mention my name?
	No one speaks.
	Oh, the Blacks are here. Sara, Virgil, hello!
SARA & **VIRGIL**	Hello, Pam.
PAM	Oh, I'm fine. Have you met Cynthia Dallas?
SARA	Yes.
VIRGIL	We've seen her perform.
PAM	Really? While I was out of the room? (*to CYNTHIA*) Were you doing some of your acting?
VIRGIL	I meant we saw her in *King Lear* last week.

PAM	Oh, of course. We saw that too. Wasn't it something!
SARA	It was a blast. Pam, I hear there's going to be food.
PAM	Here? Yes, yes. But later, when there are more people. Oh, why aren't there more people?

PAM exits abruptly.

SARA	What's wrong with us?
LEON	Nothing, I think. We're just a bit early.
SARA	We shouldn't have come at all.
LEON	Then you'd have missed the food.
SARA	But I would have got to eat dinner.
VIRGIL	So Cynthia, is this the first time you've done Shakespeare?
CYNTHIA	Well, this is the first time since I started acting professionally. I was in *Measure for Measure* at school.
VIRGIL	Oh, that's my favourite.
CYNTHIA	It used to be mine too. Now *King Lear* is my favourite.
SARA	Have you done any other Shakespeare, Cynthia?
CYNTHIA	No.
JULIUS	(*crossing to VIRGIL and handing him a glass*) Here's your drink, Virgil.
VIRGIL	Thanks. Oh. There's no cherry.
SARA	(*pulling a stem out of her mouth*) Oh. Sorry.
LEON	Sara, would you mind if I did some sketches of you?

SARA	I don't know. What would I have to do?
LEON	Just sit and talk or whatever you like. Nothing unnatural.
SARA	I suppose.
JULIUS	He's not very good you know.
SARA	That's alright. I've never modelled before.
VIRGIL	Say Cynthia, would you mind ... I wonder if ... There's a point of your interpretation of Cordelia I'd like to discuss with you.
CYNTHIA	I don't mind at all. Do you think I'm doing something wrong?
VIRGIL	Well, not wrong exactly. But there was an aspect of her character that I see just a bit differently.
CYNTHIA	Well please, tell me what it is.
VIRGIL	Alright. As I see it ...
SARA	Don't listen to him, dear. You were just fine. In fact you were the best of the lot. You carried that thing on your back.
CYNTHIA	Oh. Thank you.
SARA	Of course Cordelia is such a well-written part that it's almost a shoe-in. I've seen any number of completely stupid actresses who did just fine in the role.
LEON	Sara!
SARA	What? What ... I didn't say that she...
LEON	No, no. Just stop moving your arms. I don't want to sketch in too many.
SARA	I told you I was new at this. (*putting her hands over her breasts*) Here. This'll help me to remember.

CYNTHIA   (*to* VIRGIL) I'm still interested in what you have to say.

VIRGIL   You are. Good. It's in the first scene, the one where the other two sisters are going on about how much they love the King and you just stand there with your eyes sort of downcast, looking as though you don't know what you'll say when it's your turn.

CYNTHIA   Well that's pretty much the situation, isn't it? Cordelia doesn't know what she can say to match the speeches made by her sisters.

VIRGIL   Doesn't she? I think she deliberately sets out to make her sisters look bad by acting humble.

CYNTHIA   Well, I don't know.

VIRGIL   And everyone buys into it. The other courtiers, the audience. Everyone but the King. He sees right through her little game.

CYNTHIA   But the other sisters are wicked. They do evil things.

VIRGIL   That's later. You see, because Cordelia knows which cards to play against them, everyone comes to hate those two girls. They fall apart. They crack up. That's why the play is a tragedy.

CYNTHIA   Oh.

VIRGIL   And at the end, when the King has lost all his daughters, who does he cry over? The little sneak, the bitch, the ... I'm sorry. This is probably upsetting you.

CYNTHIA   No no. It's interesting. So you think ... hmm. How should I say my asides in the first scene? You know..."What shall Cordelia do? Love and be silent."

VIRGIL   You just have to be more offhand about the whole thing. Try saying the line and then rolling your eyes and laughing, to show that you don't mean it.

CYNTHIA   You mean like..."Then poor Cordelia ... And yet not
           so; since I am sure my love's more ponderous than my
           ... (*giggling*) ... tongue.

VIRGIL   That's it!

CYNTHIA   Actually, something about that line has always struck
           me as funny. I'll have to think this through and give it
           a try.

JULIUS   Can you do that? Just sort of change your whole
           performance?

CYNTHIA   I don't see why not. I'm not the lead and we've already
           been reviewed. Thank you so much, Mr. Black. Tell
           me, are you involved in the theatre in some way?

VIRGIL   Lord, no. I'm in the civil service.

SARA   Cynthia, take my advice and ignore my husband's.

CYNTHIA   What's your advice?

SARA   Take my ... skip it. Virgil, leave Miss Dallas alone.

CYNTHIA   It's alright, really I—

           PAM enters.

PAM   There's still no one else here. God!

LEON   Pam! What a thing to say!

PAM   What? I didn't say anything.

SARA   That's a lovely gown you're wearing, Pam.

PAM   Do you like it?

SARA   Is it yours?

PAM   Mine? Of course it's ... mine.

           PAM stares at SARA, puzzled.

SARA	Oh, Pam.

The doorbell chimes.

JULIUS & SARA	(*to themselves*) The door ...
PAM	Oh, what to do? Rita is chopping the shallots.
VIRGIL	Can't you answer the door?
PAM	Not by myself. Julius, come with me.
JULIUS	And leave the bar unattended?
PAM	Oh no, of course not. Leon?
LEON	I'm sketching.
SARA	I'm posing.
PAM	Virgil?
VIRGIL	Pam, if we answer the door together, people will assume...
PAM	Ooo.

The doorbell chimes again.

Well come on Cynthia, let's answer the door.

PAM drags CYNTHIA out.

LEON	Why can't Pam go by herself?
SARA	People are suspicious when a hostess greets them at the door. It's generally taken as a sign that things aren't going well and that she can't wait to put another log in the fire, so to speak.
VIRGIL	But isn't that actually what the situation is in this case?

SARA	Well yes. Pam is in the unenviable position of having to cover up when she actually has something to hide. But Cynthia is with her, so they can make it look like it was an accident ... Like they were just passing by when the doorbell rang.
LEON	I think Pam is afraid to answer the door because she thinks that whoever's there might shoot her.
SARA	Well, it would be her own fault. If you're going to give cocktail parties...

> *There is considerable hubbub as PAM and CYNTHIA return with four newcomers. There is a couple, DR. MAX POWELL and his wife DENISE, and two women, LILY JOHNSON and ESTELLE WASHINGTON.*

PAM	(*laughing*) Oh no, not all. Everyone else arrived just seconds ago.
VIRGIL	Max! Denise!
MAX & DENISE	Hello!
PAM	I'm sure you two remember everyone. Dr. Max Powell and Denise Powell, my husband Julius, my brother Leon, Virgil and Sara... and of course everyone knows Lily Johnson.
JULIUS	Hi Lily.
LEON	Hi Lily.
LILY	Hi Lo.
PAM	Ha ha ha. And Lily has brought her friend Estelle. Everyone, this is Estelle Washington.
ESTELLE	(*lighting a cigarette*) Hello.
JULIUS	Did you four drive down together?

DENISE	No, we just met up in the driveway. In fact, we all came in separate cars.
PAM	You and Max each drove a car?
MAX	Well, why not. We have two.

MAX and DENISE laugh.

LILY	I almost didn't make it. My car kept stalling. I'll have to get a new one.
LEON	You could have it fixed.
LILY	Why bother. I've got my eye on one of those new Ramblers.
JULIUS	Oh say!
LEON	Vroom vroom.
PAM	Estelle, let me get an ashtray for you.
ESTELLE	(*rummaging in her purse*) Actually, I've got one here. I think...
VIRGIL	(*to MAX and DENISE who are in formal attire*) You two are quite dressed up tonight.
DENISE	Yes. I hope no one minds. We're going bowling later this evening.
MAX	You're all welcome to join us. It's not a league or anything.
VIRGIL	Bowling might be strange and rather interesting. Sara?
SARA	Not tonight. I don't feel pretty enough to bowl.
JULIUS	Would any of you newcomers care for a drink?
ALL	Oh yes. Mmmm. Please, yes...

JULIUS	I've been working on something new, and I'd like everyone to try it.
PAM	Oh Julius, this isn't another of your inventions!
JULIUS	I didn't invent it.
	He lifts a tray with several small glasses of green liquid.
	It's called Hell Cocktail.
ESTELLE	Oh. Hell Cocktail! They serve that at the Savoy. It's the best (*taking a glass*) Banzai!
	She drains it.
	Woop!
PAM	Goodness!
DENISE	What's in it?
JULIUS	Never mind.
ESTELLE	(*dabbing at her forehead*) Ooo. My mind is smoking.
PAM	Julius, are you sure this is safe?
JULIUS	No. Anyone else? Max? Denise?
MAX	Oh, no thanks.
DENISE	Could I just have soda water?
JULIUS	Absolutely not.
PAM	(*to DENISE*) He's joking.
SARA	I don't think so, Pam.
LILY	Well I'll try the Hell Cocktail. I'm ready for anything.
LEON	(*to CYNTHIA*) Lily has just left her husband.

CYNTHIA	Ohh.
LILY	Cheers! (*drinks*) Zop!
JULIUS	Rah!
LILY	(*in a high-pitched voice*) It is Hell! It's Hell!
PAM	I don't think I can stand much more of this.
MAX	I beg your pardon?
PAM	(*covering her mouth*) What ... I...
DENISE	Pam?

PAM darts across to ESTELLE.

PAM	So Estelle, what do you do?
ESTELLE	I'm a divorcée.
DENISE	Leon, are you drawing something?
LEON	Yes. I'm drawing you, Denise.
DENISE	You are? Can I have a look?
LEON	If you like.
DENISE	(*examining the sketchpad*) Oh ... my. That's not quite how I see myself.
LEON	Actually, it's just your nose.
DENISE	Oh? Oh, so it is. May I have it?
LEON	If it doesn't sell.
SARA	If you're now drawing her nose, then I guess I can stop posing.
LEON	Oh yes. I'm sorry, Sara, I should have said something.

SARA	Oh, it's fine. Actually, maybe I won't stop.
	She strikes another pose.
VIRGIL	Cynthia, you're saying relatively little. You must be having an absolutely wretched time.
CYNTHIA	Oh no! This is all very interesting.
VIRGIL	Can I get you some Hell Cocktail?
CYNTHIA	Oh, no thanks. My gin is still fizzing.
VIRGIL	Yes, mine is too. I hate that.
SARA	You might get me something green to drink, Virgil dearest.
VIRGIL	Of course.
PAM	Max, you aren't drinking!
	Everyone stares at MAX.
MAX	(*sheepishly*) Oh, I'll have some sherry ... please...
JULIUS	Oh come on Max, have something stronger.
MAX	No ... No thank you...
DENISE	Hard liquor puts him right to sleep.
MAX	Honey...
JULIUS	Well you can have some sherry, but you'll have to have a lot. Is that fair? Everyone?
ALL	(*variously, nodding*) Oh yes. Absolutely. Fair's fair...
	JULIUS pours MAX an extremely large glass.
PAM	Estelle, your last name is Washington. Surely you aren't related to...
ESTELLE	To Abraham Lincoln. Why yes.

PAM   That's humorous.

ESTELLE   Yes.

SARA   (*raising a glass of Hell Cocktail*) Bonsai!

                  She drains it.

              Yow! I'll never spit again. Good work, Julius.

JULIUS   Thanks.

SARA   I'll have another. What makes it green?

JULIUS   Evil.

LEON   Lily, I must say I'm shocked by your appearance this evening.

LILY   Really why?

LEON   Your dress. It's so bright ... so ... Las Vegas ...

LILY   Oh dear.

PAM   Leon!

LEON   I didn't mean anything by that. Las Vegas is unique and exciting ... It's garish and artificial, but I didn't say it wasn't a good idea.

LILY   Oh dear.

PAM   Well I think you look fabulous, Lily.

LILY   Thank you, Pam. (*quietly*) You know. I've never worn orange before.

PAM   Really?

LILY   Yes. I was so unsure. So...unsure, but you know, I put the dress on and I looked at myself in the mirror and I thought, "Well Lily, you've got it on. You're wearing it."

PAM	(*with tremendous sympathy*) And you were right.
LILY	Thank God!
MAX	(*at a side table*) Pam, this has got to be the largest collection of napkin rings I've ever seen.
PAM	Oh, yes. Can't live without them, you know.
DENISE	We've only got eight but, my goodness, look at all of these.
JULIUS	If you count them you can find out Pam's age.
DENISE	Is that true?
PAM	No, of course it isn't. My husband is pulling on your leg.
DENISE	Oh. (*laughs*)

PAM is rather busily counting the napkin rings.

LEON	If you want to know Pam's age, you can just ask me. I'm her brother.
PAM	No! That's not true!
LEON	Pam, it is.
JULIUS	It is, Pam.
PAM	No, I mean ... I don't ... Ah ha hee. I'll just go see what's keeping Rita. She should have served delightful canapés by now.

PAM dashes out.

SARA	Canapés! That's the ticket.
LEON	Are you hungry, Sara?
SARA	Frankly, yes. Are you?

LEON	Well, yeah.
SARA	Then let's go somewhere and eat.
VIRGIL	But Sara, what of the canapés?
SARA	We'll eat them first, then we'll motor.
VIRGIL	My wife is relatively crass, isn't she?
CYNTHIA	Well...um you two seem to get along rather strangely.
VIRGIL	Now what makes you say that?
CYNTHIA	Well, she's always picking on you and putting you down.
VIRGIL	You have a very unusual way of looking at things Cynthia.
CYNTHIA	I do?
VIRGIL	Sara, Cynthia thinks we don't get along.
SARA	Who? You and me?
VIRGIL	Yes.
SARA	That's ridiculous. God!

She sits on VIRGIL's lap. They kiss passionately.

CYNTHIA	Oh.
SARA	(*stopping and looking at CYNTHIA*) God!

VIRGIL and SARA resume kissing and continue through the scene.

ESTELLE	So Max, what sort of doctor are you?
MAX	Me? I'm an ectopicologist.

ESTELLE	Sounds good. What does it mean?
MAX	I deal with congenitally displaced organs.
DENISE	He takes those ectopic organs and makes them entopic again.
ESTELLE	Is that difficult?
MAX	It's not as hard as most people think.
LILY	I don't know a thing about internal organs. Not a thing.
LEON	Are you proud of that?
JULIUS	Would anyone like another drink?
ESTELLE	Oh please.
LILY	Yes.
LEON	Two here.
CYNTHIA	Thank you, yes.

> *VIRGIL and SARA wave their arms in assent but don't stop kissing.*

MAX	I'm alright.
DENISE	No thanks. I'm ... oh heck, yes, well yes ... hee hee hee ...
JULIUS	(*rubbing his hands together gleefully*) Rah!

> *He lifts a tray containing several glasses of some bright red cocktail.*

JULIUS	Here's a round of something none of you will have tasted. I've just invented it.
LEON	What's it called?

JULIUS	I don't know. I thought we could all taste it and then think of a name.
LEON	Oh good. A fight.
JULIUS	Everyone, help yourselves.
	Mumbling and giggling, they all make their way to the bar.
	Does everyone have a glass? Then drink. Drink!
	Everyone, including VIRGIL and SARA, takes a few contemplative sips.
	What does it taste like?
SARA	The Suez Canal.
VIRGIL	Exactly.
	They resume kissing.
LEON	Absolutely not. It isn't salty at all.
ESTELLE	But it is sort of tropical and Eastern.
LILY	But not Middle-Eastern.
ESTELLE	No.
DENISE	It's sort of fruity. I'd call it Fruit Cocktail.
	She bursts out laughing.
DENISE	No, that won't do, will it?
	She continues to laugh helplessly.
JULIUS	Any more suggestions?
ESTELLE	I can't quite place it. It's west of the International Date Line ...

LILY	And sort of south but not as far as the Antipodes
LEON	Borneo?
ESTELLE	No.
LILY	And not New Guinea...

DENISE laughs some more.

ESTELLE	Isn't that silly. It's on the tip of my tongue. It's about thirteen degrees north of the equator...
MAX	Oh, that'll be Guam.
ESTELLE	That's it! Guam! Guam! It tastes like Guam!
JULIUS	(*to ESTELLE*) Have you been there?
ESTELLE	Once.
LEON	We can't just call it Guam.
LILY	Should we call it a Guam Sling or something like that?

DENISE is still laughing at her previous remark.

MAX	A Guamini?
CYNTHIA	A Guam Fizz?
ESTELLE	No. I've got it. Let's call it a Guam Slam.
ALL	Yes, yes. Bravo! Oh indeed! (*etc*)
JULIUS	A Guam Slam. Here's to that!

All clink their glasses and drink.

LEON	(*to CYNTHIA*) I was going to suggest we call it a Cynthia.
CYNTHIA	Why?

LEON	After you.
CYNTHIA	I know that, but why?
LEON	As a tribute.
CYNTHIA	I don't deserve it.
LEON	Oh Cynthia, you do. You do.
CYNTHIA	I do? Then why didn't you suggest it?
LEON	Oh, Cynthia I don't know.

> *PAM enters, followed by RITA, who carries a tray of canapés.*

PAM	Ha ha ha. Here are the canapés. Food, food. Yes, food. Ha ha ha. Rita will serve you all. Ha ha ha.
SARA	(*breaking away from VIRGIL*) Virgil, stop a minute. (*taking a canapé*) Thank you, Rita.
RITA	You're welcome.
VIRGIL	(*taking one also*) Thank you.
RITA	You're welcome.
CYNTHIA	Thank you.
RITA	Don't mention it.
LEON	Thanks, Rita.
RITA	It was no trouble at all.
LILY	Thanks.
RITA	Anytime, really.

*PAM has a quiet word with RITA, who
subsequently serves the other guests without
speaking.*

DENISE   Oh yum, thanks.

MAX   Mmm-mmm.

JULIUS   Oh, these, Rah!

PAM   No, thank you.

ESTELLE   (*taking a canapé*) Thank you. Oh. There's green pepper
on this one. I'll just trade it for one of these. Oh...

LILY   What's wrong?

ESTELLE   They all have green pepper. All of them.

PAM   Yes they do. That's what makes them special.

JULIUS   Do you not like green pepper, Estelle?

ESTELLE   (*breathing slowly, trying to remain calm*) No, I don't.
I hate it. Actually, do you want to know what I really
hate? I hate the fact that although I despise green
pepper, everyone else alive seems to love it. I mean, it
really doesn't bother me so much that I don't like the
taste, because the reasons for that are certainly either
scientific or medical. No, what bothers me is that
everyone else likes it and because they do, it is so
much in evidence.

On pizza, in salads ... The other night I found some in
stroganoff! Oh ... yuck...
And a myth has sprung up you know. People have
said to me "Well, if you don't like it, just pick it out."
But that's so stupid. Just because you pick it out,
doesn't mean the flavour's going to go away. Green
pepper doesn't work like that. It is insidious and
pervasive, like noxious fumes that kill you and your
family while you sleep. Jesus, the way some people
talk, you'd think it was parsley! I've even seen, yes it's
true, green pepper that's been sliced cross-wise to make

a sort of shamrock shaped ring. That's supposed to be decorative. Do you believe it? There's nothing like adding a garnish to make the bile really rise up in the throats of your dinner guests! (*looking around at the others who are standing quite motionless*)

Look, I know you all like green pepper and so you think I'm overreacting. But what I'm trying to say is that acceptance of these foodstuffs can never be taken for granted. You can't assume it. It's not a given. No. This is something that has caused me a lot of unhappiness and I just don't want to go through that anymore.

    Pause.

I do like red pepper though. I want you all to know that.

    The others continue to stare.

Do you think that's strange?

PAM   Well I must admit ...

ESTELLE   It's not strange! Not all!! At all!! They aren't the same, no matter what people try to tell you! They aren't!!

    She is yelling right into PAM's face.

It's like butter and margarine! Did you know that there are people in the world who think that butter and margarine taste just the same? Ha! My husband was one of them! I'll bet you're another! Well ... Well ... Obviously, some people's taste is all in their homes!

    She collapses into a chair.

PAM   (*completely tense*) Get this woman out of my house.

LILY   (*taking ESTELLE's hand*) Come on Estelle.

JULIUS   Does she really have to leave? I think she just got carried away.

PAM

Carried away? She got rude and there's no other way to put it. She'll have to leave. Maybe you ought to call the police Julius, and then she could be carried away for real.

ESTELLE

(*getting up*) That's quite alright. I can walk.

LILY

Do you want me to drive you home?

ESTELLE

No thanks, Lily. I have my car. If I can walk, I can certainly drive. You can stay here with these people and eat their green food and drink their green cocktails. Jesus! I think they're all from Mars!

ESTELLE storms out.

LILY

I'm sorry I brought her here. I didn't know, really.

JULIUS

Perhaps she's still upset from her divorce.

LILY

I don't think so. That was ten years ago.

LEON

Maybe it was some awful experience in her childhood, involving a green pepper.

PAM

Why are you all making excuses for her? Why?

PAM runs into the kitchen. The others stare after her.

CYNTHIA

Shouldn't someone see if she's alright?

JULIUS

No, I think Pam just needs to be alone.

SARA

That's for sure. She shouldn't have these parties. She should just stay in her room and not go out, ever.

CYNTHIA

Sara doesn't like your wife very much, does she?

JULIUS

(*laughing*) Are you kidding? Sara, Cynthia thinks you don't like Pam.

SARA	What? Cynthia! Pam has been my best friend for over twenty years. (*shaking her head*) God!
CYNTHIA	I ... uh
SARA	Alright, alright. I'll go and see how she's doing. I didn't think I was coming here to be tested. God!

SARA goes to the kitchen

CYNTHIA	(*to VIRGIL*) Your wife is a very complex individual Mr. Black.
VIRGIL	(*surprised*) Do you think so?
RITA	Would anyone else like one of these canapés?
MAX	Oh yes.
DENISE	Thank you.
LILY	Maybe later.
JULIUS	Just leave the tray, Rita.
RITA	Oh no. I'll need it for the next round.
JULIUS	We have other trays.
RITA	They aren't as nice as this one.
JULIUS	They're not that bad, and anyway, now that you've called attention to the fact, you might as well go ahead and use them.
RITA	(*backing away fearfully*) No. Mrs. Cochrane would ... would kill me.
LEON	She's right, Julius. Remember Eileen.

JULIUS shudders. RITA gives a little scream.

| RITA | (*briskly handing out canapés*) Look, why don't you all just take a few of these canapés. There aren't that |

many, and if you don't want to eat them now, you can just hold them until you do.

JULIUS   Well, I suppose...

RITA   (*emptying the tray*) Thanks everyone. I really appreciate this.

      RITA exits.

LEON   Well. I wonder what the next volley of canapés is going to consist of?

LILY   I hope it's not devilled ham. There is something I really can't stand.

LEON   I'd suggest you keep that to yourself.

JULIUS   I think there are to be some sort of hot hors d'oeuvres.

DENISE   Do you mean hot or hot?

MAX   Honey, what a stupid question.

DENISE   No dear. I meant...

JULIUS   I think hot.

DENISE   Oh, great. Say Leon, are you finished with my nose?

LEON   Why? Do you want it back?

      LEON laughs stupidly. CYNTHIA laughs also.

DENISE   Pardon me?

LILY   (*to LEON*) Do noses interest you?

LEON   Parts of them.

LILY   (*coquettishly*) What about mine.

LEON   (*examining her nose*) The exterior isn't much. But pharyngially... (*smacking his lips*) Yes, yes, the pharynx...

LILY	(*to MAX*) What's he talking about, Doctor?
MAX	Beats me. I'm an organ man.
LEON	I'd like to go up your lachrymal ducts, Lily. I'd like to explore them. I'd walk around in there. And you know what?
LILY	What?
LEON	I'd keep my shoes on.
LILY	Oh dear.

She crosses to the bar.

VIRGIL	Does anyone want to play charades.
ALL	No!
JULIUS	I think it's fairly rare that people actually want to play charades.
VIRGIL	Well then, is anyone willing to play?

There is a pause.

DENISE	I don't mind.
CYNTHIA	I'll play.
JULIUS	I think Pam might get really upset. She hates that sort of...activity.
LEON	Why? I mean, as long as no one is going to enjoy it ... let's play.
JULIUS	Yes, let's. Rah!
VIRGIL	Great. Should we form teams?
SARA	(*entering*) Teams? What's going on? Are we wrestling?
VIRGIL	Not this time. We're going to play charades.

SARA looks over her shoulder, raises an eyebrow and laughs once.

VIRGIL   I thought you'd be excited.

SARA   Teams are out of the question.

LEON   Definitely. We wouldn't want people to think we'd gone so far as to be actual charades enthusiasts.

SARA   Ugh, that word. It makes my blood run cold.

SARA & LEON   Enthusiasts ... (*they shiver*)

VIRGIL   Well, alright then. It'll just be every man for himself.

SARA   If you want to look at it that way. Virgil, I'm not sure you're correct in assuming anyone here actually wants to win at charades.

JULIUS   Let's just play. When we've had enough, we can stop.

The others murmur approvingly.

VIRGIL   Who'll go first?

JULIUS   How about you, Virgil? It was your idea.

VIRGIL   I don't mind.

SARA   Sorry, O.T.Q. Outta the question. To suggest the game and go first. Well, you know what that means?

SARA and LEON shiver.

Leon, you go first.

LEON   Do I have to?

SARA   Yes.

LEON   (*bounding up enthusiastically*) Hooray!

MAX   (*to LILY*) I'm finding it rather difficult to put my finger on the tone of this party.

> *LEON begins the charade preliminaries of holding up various fingers.*

SARA
JULIUS
CYNTHIA   Three words.

VIRGIL
JULIUS
CYNTHIA   First word.

DENISE   Wait a minute! Aren't there supposed to be categories, like book or movie or show tunes or whatever?

SARA   Oh Denise. Get serious!

DENISE   (*cowed*) I ... I ...

LEON   Ahem... (*holding his thumb and forefinger close together*)

VIRGIL   A little word ... A ... An ...

SARA   It.

> *LEON makes the "T" sign with his hands.*

CYNTHIA   (*excited*) The!

> *LEON touches his nose and points at CYNTHIA.*

JULIUS   She's got it! It's "The".

SARA   Go on.

> *LEON holds up two fingers.*

VIRGIL
DENISE
CYNTHIA   Second word.

LEON raises his arms which are bent at the wrists and the elbows, and moves them back and forth rigidly.

DENISE   Exercise?

MAX   Dancing?

JULIUS   I know. I know! It's Egyptian!

LEON touches his nose, points at JULIUS, and jumps up and down.

SARA   Egyptian. The Egyptian something ...

LEON holds up three fingers.

ALL   Third word!

He pauses and thinks for a moment. Then he mimes putting a crown on his head.

VIRGIL   Hat! The Egyptian Hat!

LEON shakes his head and thinks again. He raises a hand and waves decorously.

SARA   Wave! The Egyptian Wave! What?

CYNTHIA   No. I've got it! I know. I know. It's the Queen!

LEON   (*touching his nose and jumping up and down*) Yes! Yes!

CYNTHIA   The Egyptian Queen!

CYNTHIA falls into LEON's arms.

LEON   (*embracing her*) You're right! You're right! You got it right! Oh Cynthia!

LILY   I don't get it.

DENISE   Neither do I.

LEON	You haven't heard of The Egyptian Queen?
DENISE	No.
LEON	That's too bad. You must not play very often.
DENISE	No. I do. But I've never heard—
LEON	Sorry to hear it. Someone else do one.
DENISE	Well if it's all going to be a lot of obscure references then I'm not sure I want to play.
JULIUS	No one wants to play. I thought we'd established that.
VIRGIL	Denise, why don't you do the next one? Then you won't feel left out.
DENISE	Well ... I suppose ... hmmm...
SARA	Come on.
DENISE	I'm thinking. Oh! Okay. I've got one.

She moves to the centre and raises one finger.

ALL	One word!
LEON	If?
JULIUS	And!
SARA	Let her do it.

DENISE sticks out her neck and flaps her arms.

ALL	Bird!
DENISE	(*ecstatically*) Yes!
LEON	Great charade, Denise.
SARA	Yeah, really.
MAX	(*embracing DENISE*) I'm proud of you, babe.

DENISE covers her face with her hands.

SARA   Babe?

JULIUS   Babe?

LEON   I guess that makes him Paul Bunyan.

            SARA, JULIUS, and LEON laugh hysterically.
            They lie in a heap on the floor.

SARA   Oh God. Oh God. Oh God ...

VIRGIL   Let's have another charade.

DENISE   Yes, let's. What's so funny. Was it my bird imitation?

VIRGIL   I don't think so. Cynthia, why don't you do the next
            one?

CYNTHIA   Oh, no ...

LILY   Oh, yes, do.

SARA   (*still on the floor*) Come on. You're an actress. This
            should be a piece of cake for you.

CYNTHIA   But usually I just act with my mouth.

            JULIUS, LEON and SARA laugh some more.

            I mean verbally. Well, what the heck. I'll try.

JULIUS   Rah!

            CYNTHIA crosses to the centre. She stands for a
            moment, then raises her hand.

SARA
LEON
VIRGIL   Five words.

LEON
VIRGIL   First word.

SARA   A short word. A ... an...

> *CYNTHIA makes the "T" sign.*

LEON
LILY   The!

> *CYNTHIA touches her nose, then resumes, holding up three fingers.*

MAX
LILY
JULIUS   Second word.

JULIUS   Whoops, third word.

SARA   She's going out of sequence.

LEON   Cynthia, you're wild!

CYNTHIA   Thanks. (*making the small word sign*)

SARA   Another small word. A ... An

LILY   But.

MAX   If.

DENISE   The.

LEON   It! It!

> *CYNTHIA puts her hands on her hips and stares at the others with mock sternness. She makes alphabet signs until she reaches "O'.*

JULIUS   O ... on...

LILY   Or...

MAX   Of?

            CYNTHIA touches her nose, points at MAX and emits a piercing shriek.

LEON   I think that means yes.

SARA   The hm of hm hm ... Hmmmm

            CYNTHIA holds up four fingers.

DENISE   Fourth word.

SARA   Well du-uh.

LEON   (*running his hands through his hair*) God this is exciting!

JULIUS   Leon!

            CYNTHIA makes the "I" sign.

ALL   The!

            CYNTHIA bursts out laughing.

SARA   Cynthia!

CYNTHIA   (*touching her nose*) Sorry.

LILY   The hm of the hm I know! *The Hound of the Baskervilles!* I'll bet that last word would have been a challenge.

CYNTHIA   Not at all. Anyway, you're wrong, Lily.

LILY   Oh poop. (*covering her mouth*)

JULIUS   Is it *The Wreck of the Hesperus*?

CYNTHIA   Oh, that would have been a good one. No, it's not.

SARA   Just let her do the rest of the words. Go on, Cynthia.

            CYNTHIA holds up five fingers.

VIRGIL	Fifth word.

> *CYNTHIA thinks for a moment, then gestures broadly about.*

DENISE	Large...
LEON	Wide...
SARA	Everything...

> *CYNTHIA stops. She thinks again and gestures to her ear.*

LEON & JULIUS	Sounds like...

> *CYNTHIA leaps around clapping her hands. She mimes blowing up balloons and throwing streamers.*

SARA	(*after a moment*) This seems a little indulgent.
LEON	Are you some sort of party?

> *CYNTHIA nods enthusiastically.*

Party? Festivity? Festive? It's festival? What are you celebrating?

> *CYNTHIA screams.*

Celebrating? Celebrate. Celebrity? What?

LILY	Celebration?

> *CYNTHIA screams again.*

I got it. I got it. It's a celebration.

LEON	No it isn't!
LILY	But...
LEON	This is a "sounds like". Remember?

LILY	Oh, right.
JULIUS	Sounds like "celebration"?
MAX	Coordination?
DENISE	Vibration?

> *CYNTHIA shakes her head. She does the alphabet up to "N".*

LEON	N! N! Nelebration ... That's not really a word, Cynthia.
SARA	It certainly isn't. You lose. Forfeit your turn. Get lost.
DENISE	Is it maybe ... just ... nation

> *Everyone turns and glares at DENISE.*

CYNTHIA	(*after a pause*) Well ... yes.

> *Everyone turns and glares at CYNTHIA.*

DENISE	The hm of a Nation...
VIRGIL	Well, obviously it's *The B*—
SARA	(*clapping a hand over his mouth*) Wait! I want to see her do the second word.
CYNTHIA	(*hands on hips*) Oh!
LEON	Go on, Cynthia.
JULIUS	You can do it.
VIRGIL	This is ridiculous. There's no need to embarrass her. I know the answer. It's *The Bi*—

> *SARA throws herself on VIRGIL and kisses him. CYNTHIA sighs and holds up two fingers.*

ALL   (*except VIRGIL and SARA*) Second word!

CYNTHIA   Well, I guess I set myself up for this one.

                     *She lies down on her back with her knees apart
                     and starts making extraordinary facial contortions
                     and even groans a little.*

DENISE   Oh.

LILY   My.

                     *CYNTHIA makes muffled cries, SARA breaks
                     away from VIRGIL.*

SARA   Sound effects. I love it.

MAX   I have no idea what this is meant to represent.

                     *PAM enters followed by RITA, who carries a tray
                     of hors d'ouevres. They both stop in their tracks
                     and stare at CYNTHIA.*

PAM   Cynthia! My God, what's happening!

                     *RITA drops her tray and begins screaming
                     enthusiastically.*

                     Rita! Stop screaming!

                     RITA stops.

PAM   (*to RITA*) Phone the police! Call an ambulance!

                     *RITA turns to go but is stopped by JULIUS,
                     PAM kneels beside CYNTHIA.*

                     Cynthia, Cynthia ... When I invited you here, I had no
                     idea you were a diabetic ...or whatever. But it's alright.
                     You'll be fine. Oh, my nerves. Someone get a blanket.
                     Poor Cynthia.

                     CYNTHIA has started to shake with laughter.

Oh ... Why are you laughing? Is this hysteria? Help!
Help!! She's hysterical!!

CYNTHIA   (*still laughing*) No, no. Pam! I'm quite alright. It's
               just I mean ... I'm ... Oh...

PAM   What on earth... (*looking around*) And why is
               everyone else laughing?

               Everyone in the room is laughing uproariously.

               You're laughing at me! At meeee!

LEON   Oh, Pam. Pam, Pam...

SARA   You've been fooled.

VIRGIL   We were playing a game.

JULIUS   Cynthia was doing a charade.

PAM   A charade. A charade in my home? At my cocktail
               party. Oh ... I ... Do you mean to say that the minute
               I turn my back, you all start to play party games? To
               have cheap competitive fun?

               She is lurching across the room.

               First that woman comes in here and insults my food,
               my home, and ... and me and now this happens?
               This—

               She is close to choking.

LEON   Aw come on, Pam. It was just charades. You used to
               play all the time.

PAM   When I was eight, yes!

JULIUS   We didn't form teams.

VIRGIL   We weren't competing. That's the honest truth.

DENISE	Yes, we were just playing for fun ... To enjoy ourselves.
SARA	Denise! You know that's not true. No one was enjoying anything!
PAM	Oh really? Is that a fact? Then I've failed have I? I've failed!
SARA	No, Pam, you haven't. You've just done what you always do.
PAM	What?
SARA	You've always assumed that we were enjoying ourselves at your parties. I suppose you'd have to do this in order to go on giving them, but the fact is they aren't really much fun, and they never have been. Why do we come then? Well, why do we play charades even though we hate the game? Because it's inevitable. And your parties are inevitable, and everything in our lives is inevitable, so why not get out of the house every now and again.
PAM	Sara ... I never knew ... You ... My best friend. All along you've been hating these parties. These parties where I was truly content...
SARA	I've never held it against you, Pam. It's always been a bit of a hoot to watch you at these ordeals. You've always seemed to be happy and I've found that amusing.
PAM	WELL DO YOU THINK I'M HAPPY NOW??? DO YOU??

She turns on the other guests, her eyes flashing.

PAM	What about the rest of you? Do you enjoy my parties?
DENISE	Oh, yes.
MAX	We do...

PAM   I DON'T BELIEVE YOU!!!

LILY   Well they can be a bit stuffy. I mean, there always
               seem to be things you can't say or do?

PAM   Well why did you bring a total stranger here then, if
               this is such a living hell?

LILY   I thought someone new might liven the party up. One
               so often sees the same faces here. Oh ... no offence
               everyone.

JULIUS   None taken. I know just what you mean. We have
               these parties just about every month, but they all seem
               to run together into one big one because each one is
               exactly like the last. And even if the people are
               different, it doesn't matter because they all talk about
               the same things anyway.

PAM   But that's the point. There's such stability and
               permanence. Doesn't anyone else need those things?

VIRGIL   Not really, Pam. We all have jobs.

PAM   Oh ...

               *PAM stands very still, with her mouth slightly
               open.*

CYNTHIA   (*after a pause*) I really must say that I've had a very
               nice time here.

               Trembling violently, PAM turns to CYNTHIA.

PAM   You certainly have! Staging fits in my living room!
               This is all your fault! I'll bet you're in cahoots with
               that woman! That hideous evil divorcée!!!

LEON   Pam! Don't yell at Cynthia.

PAM   Oh, sorry. I might upset her, is that it? Is that it?!!!

               *PAM takes a sudden step backward, trips and falls
               on the floor.*

PAM   Ow! Oh! Oh my God! What are these? They're canapés! I'm sitting in the hot hors d'oeuvres. What are they doing on the floor? They're ruined! Ruined!! Rita? RITA!! They're not even hot anymore!!!

                     PAM is crawling about on the floor, gasping and shrieking.

                     How can I serve these? And why would I want to? To these people. These boors! Taking advantage of my hospitality ... hospitality.

                     Food. Drinks ... Hostess ... Canapés ... Cana ... Ahhhhhhh.

                     She falls on her face and lies very still.

SARA   Pam? Are you ... Oh no.

DENISE   Someone, do something.

LEON   (*looking at DENISE*) What?

MAX   Julius, you're her husband.

JULIUS   So?

LILY   Rita?

                     RITA backs away. PAM slowly raises her head. She has a strange, rather foggy expression.

PAM   And who are ye all? Why do ye stare so? (*to CYNTHIA*) Tell me lassie, whut's amuck?

LEON   Oh my...

VIRGIL   Madness.

SARA   Poor Pam. Poor, poor Pam.

PAM   (*laughing like a child*) Saw ye ne'er in yer life sae dainty a chamber o'deas. See as the moon shines down sae caller a the fresh strae. (*whimpering*) Ah, wae's me. Wae's me. (*tugging MAX's pantleg*)

PAM But tell me ... Were ye ever in Bedlam?

MAX No. Never.

He pulls away from PAM, who gets up and skips about.

PAM There's no pleasanter cell in Bedlam, braw a place as it is on the outside ... (*stopping suddenly*) Mine sheep? Now, where be mine ain sheep? (*wandering around*) Sheep ... Sheepsheepsheep, Baa-baa-baa ...

SARA This is awful. Julius, has this happened before?

JULIUS Not that I recall.

SARA Leon, what about when you were growing up? Did she ever...

LEON Not at all. She's always been just how she was. I'm kind of impressed.

The doorbell rings.

JULIUS & SARA The door.

PAM Ho ho. Bells! Did ye hear everyone? Those be my wedding bells? But where be my bonny bridegroom. And where mine sheep? Alack a-day ... Alack.

VIRGIL Should someone answer the door?

SARA Yes. Rita, would you get it please? Julius, help me to get Pam out of here. I don't think anyone should see her in this condition.

JULIUS Of course. (*taking PAM's arm*) Come on Pam...

PAM (*hotly*) Nae rinthercout! Be off wi ye or I'll haena swither to jagg ye in the kail!

JULIUS (*leaping back*) Yikes!

SARA   Pam, you've got to come with me now.

              She is leading PAM by the hand.

              Come. Come to the church.

              The doorbell rings again.

              Do you hear. Wedding bells.

PAM   Aye aye. Let us to the fane.

              *She turns abruptly and addresses the others with a
              snarl.*

              Binna ye not uncauteelous. I hae planked a chury!

              She laughs maniacally and drags SARA away.

SARA   (*as they go*) A chury! a chury!

              Everyone stares for a moment.

CYNTHIA   Gosh.

RITA   Should I get the door now?

JULIUS   I suppose you'd better.
              RITA goes.

LILY   What are we going to do? Max, you're a doctor. There
              must be something you can suggest.

MAX   I...um. I really don't think so.

LEON   I doubt whether Pam's affliction has a whole lot to do
              with her duodenum.

DENISE   I think we should leave.

LILY   What? Just walk out?

DENISE Yes, why not? We're just guests. I don't think we should be held responsible for the way the hostess behaves.

LEON She's sick.

DENISE Well then all the more reason to leave. If she's sick then she obviously doesn't need a houseful of guests.

RITA enters, followed by ESTELLE.

RITA Mrs. Washington has come back.

JULIUS Oh no!

LEON Oh-oh.

LILY Estelle, what are you doing here?

ESTELLE I came back to apologize. I think I behaved badly. I've been sitting in my car thinking, and I've decided that my reaction was extreme and uncalled-for. I want to tell Pam that I'm sorry.

JULIUS You can't.

LILY It's too late.

ESTELLE Oh, don't you all start in on me too. This hasn't been easy. It's taken me all this time to be able to turn around and face the house again. But I did, and since I didn't turn into a pillar of salt. I knew I'd made the right decision.

>*She laughs nervously and looks around at the others.*

Is something wrong? Is something going on? Somebody answer me. Where's Pam? I just want to see her for a minute and then I'll go.

>*Pause.*

ESTELLE	What's happening here? Somebody, tell me! Lily? (*shaking LILY*) Lily, what's happened to Pam!
LILY	She's ... No, I can't say it ... Oh, Estelle...
ESTELLE	What? What?
LILY	It's not your fault, Estelle! Please believe me! There were other factors. It's not your fault. I want you to understand that. Please!
ESTELLE	Understand what? What are you talking about?
LILY	Pam ... she's...

> *PAM dashes into the room. She's wearing a nightgown and her hair is about her ears. She's cackling ferociously and is followed closely by SARA.*

ESTELLE	(*aghast*) Oh Lord!
PAM	Flat birkies! Ha ha ha! (*to DENISE*) Ye maun pickle in thine ain pokenook!

> *DENISE bursts into tears. MAX embraces her stoically.*

ESTELLE	She's lost her mind.
LEON	Well, yeah!
PAM	(*approaching ESTELLE, grinning lewdly*) How now? How now, sauce-box?

> *ESTELLE turns away.*

PAM	What say ye now, Miss Pert?

> *She stares at ESTELLE with fierce intensity.*

SARA	(*hoarsely, to LEON*) What's that woman doing here?
LEON	She came back to apologize.

SARA   (*covering her face with one hand*) What makes people
            do that sort of thing?

ESTELLE   (*to PAM*) Pam, I just want you to know... I'm very
            sorry for what I said earlier The way I behaved...If
            there's anything I can do...

            She breaks down and sobs.

PAM   (*embracing ESTELLE*) Nay, nay chucky. Be ye blithe,
            be ye blithe. Will ye have a mutchkin o'usquebaugh?

            *ESTELLE looks at PAM uncomprehendingly.
            PAM picks up some half empty cocktail glasses
            and pours them into one glass. She offers it to
            ESTELLE who shakes her head and pulls back.*

            Ach! Daft cuthy!

            *PAM downs the contents of the glass, wipes her
            mouth with her hand and then belches.*

            Now I maun take me tap in me lap!

            PAM runs to the door, then turns abruptly.

PAM   But beware! Beware St. Nicholas Clarks. I mauna gane
            cause I haena skeel o'the gate.

            *Feeling the effects of the alcohol, she lurches and
            staggers.*

            Wae ... Wae ... Eee...

            She falls on her face.

SARA   (*after a pause*) Is she conscious?

LILY   She's breathing, I can see that.

LEON   Julius, let's help her up.

> *LEON and JULIUS lift PAM and put her in a chair.*

JULIUS What should we do now?

LILY Bathe her temples.

VIRGIL Rub her palms.

RITA Tweak her nose.

> *PAM groans loudly and opens her eyes a little.*

PAM Where am I? Oh, Julius ... Is that you?

JULIUS Yes Pam, It's me. It's me. Pam, you've come back to us.

PAM Oh Julius, I've felt so strange.

> *She sits up slowly and embraces JULIUS.*

LEON Pam, Pam, thank God you're alright.

> *Still holding JULIUS, PAM opens her eyes and sees the others all gathered round.*

PAM I ... What? All these people ... What are they doing here? Oh my God! I'M WEARING A NIGHTGOWN!!!

> *PAM utters a piercing shriek and starts running about the room roaring and snorting and jumping over the furniture.*

SARA Oh, no.

LEON Look out!

LILY Eeek!

> *The others run hither and thither trying to keep out of PAM's way. They exit en masse through one door and she follows them off. The stage is*

> *empty for a moment before Pam pursues the*
> *ghosts back on through another door.*

PAM   (*standing on the couch, singing loudly*) "Oh I am king of the forest..."

> *She dives on top of SARA.*

SARA   Ough!

PAM   Come. Away with me to the forest. We'll live among the poplars. We'll catch squirrels and skin 'em and eat 'em.

SARA   Oh yuck. This is going too far.

PAM   (*dragging SARA by the hand*) Come on!

VIRGIL   Go with her, Sara. See where she wants to take you.

ESTELLE   Fresh air might do her some good.

SARA   Don't let her take me too far. Pam, you're in your bare feet.

PAM   Bare feet? Bare feet!! (*laughing*) Then we'll away to Palestine!!

> *PAM drags SARA away. Everyone watches them*
> *go. There is a very long pause.*

JULIUS   Well, would anyone like a drink?

> *There is a loud commotion as everyone heads*
> *directly for the bar. JULIUS puts out bottles and*
> *glasses and everyone helps themselves rather*
> *liberally.*

CYNTHIA   Where do you think they'll go?

JULIUS   I don't know. There's lots of countryside around here.

DENISE   Aren't you concerned?

JULIUS	Concerned? About?
LILY	I suppose she'll be looking for sheep.
LEON	No, I think she's out of that phase. But think of it. Pam among sheep. *LEON and JULIUS laugh.*
MAX	I think someone ought to notify the police or the Mounties or someone.
JULIUS	Why? If we bring the law into this it'll only risk driving her further over the brink. You saw what happened when she saw us all staring at her, and we're her friends ... I'm her husband for corn's sake!
VIRGIL	That's true. Leave her alone and she'll come home.
LEON	Dragging your wife behind her.
MAX	Well when she does come home, I think you ought to take some fairly decisive steps. The woman is unhinged. She needs a doctor's care. She should be put in an institution. She's dangerous.
JULIUS	Max, I think you're overreacting. You saw Pam as she left. She was happy. She was inspired.
VIRGIL	That's right, you know. It's like *King Lear*, when he goes mad. He's so much happier, innocent and unburdened by cares. Isn't that right, Cynthia?
CYNTHIA	I don't know, I'm not in that part of the play.
VIRGIL	Even Lady Macbeth is less of a threat once she gets a bit askew.
MAX	Are you suggesting Pam was a threat?
VIRGIL	Not a threat so much as intimidating.
JULIUS	Yes, I think that's a good way of putting it.

MAX	Well I don't know why you'd all keep coming to her parties, disliking her as you do. I'm really truly amazed by the hypocrisy here. You're all hypocrites.
DENISE	Yeah!
LEON	Oh come on, Denise ... You knew how Pam felt about charades and that didn't stop you from...

He does DENISE's bird imitation.

MAX	Is that supposed to be my wife?
LEON	I think it was a bird imitation.
MAX	But it was my wife doing a bird imitation, wasn't it? And it wasn't very flattering!
DENISE	Max, it's okay. He does have a point. We did play charades and we really shouldn't have.
MAX	Stay out of this, babe. (*to LEON*) No one does imitations of my wife!

MAX raises his fists. DENISE and CYNTHIA gasp and put there hands to their mouths.

LEON	That's what you think. People are always imitating her. See, Cynthia's doing her now.
CYNTHIA	(*dropping her hands*) No. I ...
DENISE	Hmmmmph!
MAX	That's it. Come on, bub, let's fight.
LEON	(*waving his fists*) If you will, jackanapes!
JULIUS	I have a better idea. Max, why don't you and your wife just get out of my house?
LEON	Don't you have to go bowling. (*patting MAX on the chest*) We'll fight some other time, I'll dress up too and then it'll be more fair.

MAX	Why you...
DENISE	Max, let's just go. You can play some pinball first and that'll calm you down.
JULIUS	Yeah, go, go.
MAX	We're going.
DENISE	Good-bye, Lily. Good-bye Estelle. It was nice meeting you.
ESTELLE	Bye.

MAX and DENISE exit quickly.

JULIUS	I've always hated that couple.
LEON	So have I.

LEON and JULIUS make faces at the door.

ESTELLE	You know, at the risk of seeming rude, I'm afraid I'm going to have to excuse myself as well. You see, I'm expecting guests in my home at some point in the future and I really ought to vacuum.

She runs out.

LEON	That's an interesting way of leaving a party.
LILY	I wouldn't be surprised if Estelle was feeling a bit uncomfortable here. Maybe I should go with her. Oh! I have to go with her. My car will never make it. Estelle! Estelle wait ...

LILY runs out.

JULIUS	Has no one ever heard of saying good-bye?
LEON	Well Cynthia, how about you? Do you have to go too?

CYNTHIA   Not really. Oh, should I? Would that be appropriate. I mean if it's time to go I'll go. I don't know all the rules ...

JULIUS   So make them up. You're welcome to stay.

CYNTHIA   Oh good. I don't have anything else to do.

LEON   Poor Cynthia.

CYNTHIA   Oh no. I'm alright, and I am curious to find out what's become of Pam.

LEON   I wonder if there are any other guests coming.

JULIUS   I'm sure I don't know.

LEON   Cynthia, you're not expecting anyone? A ride? A date?

CYNTHIA   Oh no.

LEON   No?

CYNTHIA   I don't think so.

LEON   Oh, Cynthia.

CYNTHIA   What?

LEON   What? What?

CYNTHIA   What?

SARA enters, panting a bit and carrying her shoes.

VIRGIL   Sara!

LEON   Where's Pam?

CYNTHIA   Yes, what's happened to Pam?

SARA   I'm out of breath. Give me a cigarette.

> *Everyone fumbles in their pockets. VIRGIL*
> *produces a cigarette.*

VIRGIL Here you are, Sara.

SARA Light it.

VIRGIL Of course.

> *He lights it. She inhales deeply.*

SARA Great, thanks.

LEON Now tell us where Pam is.

SARA I was about to. Julius, sit down.

JULIUS (*sitting*) Alright.

LEON Should we all sit?

SARA I don't care.

VIRGIL Tell us the news.

SARA (*putting a hand on JULIUS' shoulder*) Pam is gone.
She is ... gone.

JULIUS What? Dead?

SARA No, not dead. Gone! Vamoosed. Fled for parts
unknown.

VIRGIL You mean she ran away?

SARA Better ... I mean ... worse? She got a ride.

JULIUS A ride? With Max and Denise?

SARA No. (*looking around*) Oh, have they gone? Good. No.
Pam was picked up by an enormous truck.

JULIUS Pam? In a truck?
> *He bursts out laughing. LEON laughs also.*

SARA   Yes. After we left here, she dragged me through those
             woods out front across that little field that ends with
             the hill leading down to the highway. She let go of me
             finally, and then she climbs over this chicken wire
             fence, falls off it onto the hill and rolls down into the
             ditch. I thought she'd be a goner for sure, but she just
             jumped to her feet and started waving at cars. She was
             quite a spectacle in that frilly nightgown. A lot of
             drivers honked their horns, but none of them stopped.

VIRGIL   Did you go after her?

SARA   In this get-up? I'd have had to roll down as well and I
             wasn't about to do that. I'm not crazy. Oh, sorry
             Julius, no offence.

JULIUS   None taken. But tell us about the truck.

SARA   There's not much to say. She'd been hopping around
             for a while and finally this big freight truck came
             along, probably five, six tons ... Pam was waving
             away and the guy pulls over, stops, the door opens, in
             she gets and off they go.

VIRGIL   Did you get the license number?

SARA   No, there were too many plates. Many plates of many
             states.

JULIUS   I wonder if we'll ever see her again.

SARA   You know, I doubt it.

CYNTHIA   Will you miss her, Julius?

JULIUS   How should I know? She's never been away before.

SARA   Let's not dwell on it.

JULIUS   Indeed, let's not. Can I get anyone a drink? Cynthia,
             Gin Fizz?

CYNTHIA   Oh, yes please.

LEON	And another for me.
JULIUS	And another and another. Sara, anything for you?
SARA	Exactly.
	JULIUS goes to the bar and begins to mix drinks.
JULIUS	And please, converse amongst yourselves.
	Everyone looks a little perplexed.
VIRGIL	(*after a pause*) Oh say! We heard the most fascinating radio play in the car on the way out here.
SARA	If you like radio plays. "Over here. Over there. Slam! Whoosh! Caw! Caw!"
VIRGIL	Sara, this one wasn't like that at all.
JULIUS	What was it about?
VIRGIL	It was about the creation of the world, as seen from the Finnish perspective.
SARA	It was malarkey.
VIRGIL	It was mythical.
SARA	That's what I meant.
CYNTHIA	Wait a second! Was that the one about the virgin of the air and the thing that laid the egg on her knee after she swam through the uncharted waters of the unformed earth?
VIRGIL	Yes, exactly.
CYNTHIA	Well for heaven's sake. I was in that radio play.
VIRGIL	No!
CYNTHIA	Yes, I was the virgin.

SARA   No!

CYNTHIA   I was. I was. We recorded it last month.

JULIUS   I'm curious. You said something laid an egg on her knee. What was the thing?

CYNTHIA   It was a teal.

JULIUS   A teal? Now what exactly is a teal?

CYNTHIA   It's a kind of bird.

SARA   It's a seagull.

LEON   No no. It's like a duck.

VIRGIL   Wait a second. A bird? I thought a teal was like an otter.

SARA   An otter? The thing flew around, remember? It flew through the air, looking for a place to build its nest.

VIRGIL   But it was a myth. I figure otters can do pretty much as they please in myths.

SARA   Perhaps they can, but this myth is about a teal and everyone knows that teal is just another word for seagull. So there. Die.

LEON   Sara, I think the word you're looking for is tern.

SARA   I wasn't looking for a word, Leon.

VIRGIL   Why don't we ask Cynthia? She was in the play.

CYNTHIA   Oh, well I didn't actually see it. It was a sound effect.

LEON   A sound effect like a duck I'll bet.

SARA   Like a duck? There is nothing like a duck. Either you are one or you aren't. Nothing else.

CYNTHIA	What about a goose?
SARA	A goose is nothing like a duck. What's wrong with you people?
LEON	A teal is like a duck. I swear it. (*kneeling*) On my knees. (*lying down*) On my face. Please believe me Sara. Please.
VIRGIL	Well what's like an otter then?
SARA	It doesn't matter about otters. The thing in the story laid an egg so it could not have been an otter.
VIRGIL	But there is that egg-laying mammal in Australia...
SARA	We aren't talking about Australia! This was about Finland for crying out loud! FIN! LAND!
VIRGIL	That doesn't mean ...
SARA	FOR GOD'S SAKE VIRGIL, SHUT UP!!
	She pins him down and kisses him.
CYNTHIA	(*after a moment*) Well I guess that about settles –
LEON	FOR GOD'S SAKE CYNTHIA, SHUT UP!!!
	He grabs her and kisses her. They pull apart after a moment.
CYNTHIA	Leon! What...
LEON	What? What?
	LEON and CYNTHIA stare at one another in intense confusion. VIRGIL and SARA continue kissing. RITA sits on a stool beside the bar, where she's been drinking continuously since PAM's departure. JULIUS comes forward with a tray of drinks.
JULIUS	Well, here we are. Oh ... (after *standing back and observing the two couples, who are quite oblivious to*

their surroundings, he crosses back to the bar and puts the tray next to RITA) I guess these'll all be for us.

RITA   *(putting down an empty glass and taking a full one)* That'sh shooper...

> *JULIUS takes a cocktail, has a sip and surveys the room again.*

JULIUS   Now Rita, you might think it's pretty much the apex of rudeness for people to ignore their host in this way.

> *RITA nods, slowly and seriously.*

But I think I'm going to go to bed while I still have guests in my home, and that's pretty much indefensible as well.

RITA   *(rocking slowly)* Mmm

JULIUS   But the thing is, I do have to work tomorrow.

RITA   Mmm-hmm.

JULIUS   Perhaps though, since you're still here ... you might join me in a little toast. I think it only fitting that we salute our hostess, because after all, if not for her initiative, none of us would have spent this evening in quite the way that we did.

> *RITA raises her glass with some difficulty.*

Fond regards and best wishes then, to my absent wife...

> *He clinks his glass against RITA's. This slight pressure unbalances her and she teeters precariously. JULIUS only has time to take her glass from her hand as she slides off the stool and falls into a heap on the floor. JULIUS looks at her and then at the glasses he holds in each hand.*

To Pam.

> *He clinks the two glasses together and smiles. The End. Blackout.*

"Evelyn Strange" was first presented by Teatro La Quindicina at the Varscona Theatre in Edmonton, November 9 to 25, 1995, with the following cast:.

NINA FERRER	*Davina Stewart*
PERRY SPANGLER	*John Kirkpatrick*
EVELYN STRANGE	*Jane Spidell*
LEWIS HAKE	*Jeff Haslam*

Produced by Stewart Lemoine.
Set, lighting and costume design by Roger Schultz.
Stage manager - Leslea Kroll.

Playwright's Note

Our production of "Evelyn Strange" made copious use of the music of Wagner's "Siegfried", and I would expect that any other production would do the same. There are two important reasons for this. One is that its presence reinforces the identification Perry and Evelyn feel with the questing characters of Siegfried and Brunhilde. The other is that these lush torrents of sound have a similar impact to that of the outsize romanticism of Bernard Herman's score for Hitchcock's "Vertigo". This is entirely appropriate since the characters and visual style of "Evelyn Strange" stand as something of an homage to this great film. I've noted in the body of the play those excerpts which I think are specific and crucial, and I'd recommend more "Siegfried" during scene changes and blackouts as well. As Nina Ferrer would no doubt point out, there's quite a bit of music from which to choose.

Act One, Scene One

*The Metropolitan Opera, New York City. It is
just before curtain time on an autumn evening in
1955. NINA FERRER, elegantly gowned and
coifed, sits in one of the front seats of a box on
the Grand Tier. There is an empty seat beside her
and two behind. She is checking her watch and
looking down below when PERRY SPANGLER
enters the rear of the box He's wearing a dark suit.*

PERRY   Mrs. Ferrer?

NINA   *(turning)* Oh, Perry, for heaven's sake! What a pleasant
surprise.

PERRY   How are you, Nina?

NINA   I'm very well. I'm just waiting for Henry, as usual. He
should be along shortly. I'm convinced of this because
it's only a few minutes before curtain.

PERRY   Actually, Nina, you're not waiting for your husband at
all. In fact, you've been waiting for me and you just
didn't know it.

NINA   I beg your pardon.

PERRY   Henry gave me his ticket. He popped his head into my
office just before five and said he had to attend a
meeting unexpectedly, and he wouldn't be done in time
to come here. He asked me to be your escort this
evening and to see that you make your train alright
when the opera's over.

NINA   Did he tell you to wake me at the intermissions?

PERRY   No. Well, yes. He's entrusted me with a note for you.

He hands her a note which she peruses quickly,
raising her eyebrows only slightly.

PERRY   I'm sorry Nina, I think you'd already have left
        Westchester by the time he found out, so he couldn't—

NINA   Perry, please...I'm not upset. I'm glad he sent someone
        and I'm glad it's you.

PERRY   I'm surprised that it's me actually. I thought he'd have
        asked Lewis Hake.

NINA   Oh? And why is that?

PERRY   Well, he's just that much more of the man about town
        than I am. I should think he'd be more at home here
        on the Grand Tier.

NINA   Nonsense. And from what little I know of Mr. Hake's
        reputation, his social calendar is unlikely to allow for
        last-minute invitations. It would more than likely
        mean dislodging an important stewardess. Now sit
        down, Perry. "Siegfried" is about to begin and we
        must make ready.

PERRY   (*sitting beside her*) How do we do that?

NINA   Well you can read your programme synopsis, of
        course, but I also find with the music dramas of
        Wagner it's best to practice breathing as slowly as
        possible so you can lower your heart rate.

PERRY   I'm going to go out on a limb and speculate that this
        isn't your favourite opera.

NINA   I confess I haven't actually seen it before. I've heard it
        on the radio a few times on Saturday afternoons and
        it's always been one of those "My God, is that still
        on?" propositions.

PERRY   The story always seemed rather appealing to me. The
        lad slaying the dragon with his magic sword and
        waking the sleeping maiden and delivering her from
        the ring of fire.

NINA	Yes, but it just takes such a profoundly long time for him to get it all done.
PERRY	I don't think five hours is unreasonable when you consider the obstacles.
NINA	Maybe not. And I'm hoping to conquer something myself tonight.
PERRY	And what's that?
NINA	It's a recurring fear I've had at every other opera or ballet or play that I've been to. I always sit in my seat before the curtain and I'm convinced that there will be an announcement to the effect that "Ladies and Gentlemen, this evening's performance of "Abie's Irish Rose" has been cancelled. In it's place..."Siegfried". "Naughty Marietta" will not be seen tonight ... Kindly accept ... "Siegfried". And there I'd be trapped.
PERRY	Maybe you'll be lucky and there'll be an announcement like that tonight.
NINA	"We regret that this evening's performance of "Siegfried" will not take place. Instead, we offer last week's performance of "Siegfried"."
PERRY	You know, I'm starting to be a little amazed that you're here at all.
NINA	But my dear, we have tickets. We've a box for the season. I clawed my way out of obscurity just to sit in this seat.
PERRY	You were obscure?
NINA	Completely. I was a little little person who worked hard all the time.
PERRY	What did you do?
NINA	I don't remember. What does it matter, now that I'm here in a box?

PERRY   I haven't sat in a box before. I usually stand or sit up in the stratosphere.

NINA   I find it's worth the extra money to have some privacy. In case you need to contort.

PERRY   No one's sitting in these other two seats?

NINA   Not tonight, evidently.

The lights begin to lower and applause is heard.

Ah, here comes the conductor.

PERRY   He's a bit of an oldster.

NINA   I hope he makes it. (*sighing*) It's all so cruel. Well, I guess I'll see you later.

She turns to face the stage. They stare ahead as the quietly ominous prelude to "Siegfried" is heard. After a few moments, EVELYN STRANGE slips into the rear of the box. She stands in the shadows for a moment, then comes slowly forward. She's wearing a dark suit and has a light-coloured raincoat over her arm. PERRY senses her presence and turns his head a little to see her. EVELYN gives an apologetic little nod, then sits quickly and quietly in one of the rear seats. PERRY glances at NINA, who continues to stare ahead in a concentrated fashion. He returns his attention to the stage as the light fades.

Act One, Scene Two

As the lights come up at the end of the first act of "Siegfried". PERRY and NINA are applauding politely. EVELYN is no longer seated in the box. PERRY turns back and is a bit surprised by this.

PERRY   Oh. That's odd.

NINA   What is?

PERRY   There was a woman sitting behind us, but now she's gone. She came in quietly just at the start.

NINA   Really? I didn't notice.

PERRY   Yes, you certainly seemed to be following the opera rather intently.

NINA   Is that how it looked? Good.

PERRY   How are you enjoying it actually?

NINA   Perry, I'll be succinct. I don't think I can stand to hear another note of this. If I don't walk away right now, I'm afraid I'll be leaving on a stretcher.

PERRY   Do you want to go outside and get some air?

NINA   I want to go home. I want to go home and have a bath and go to bed, and I don't think I can wait another three and a half hours to do it. Four and a half when you add the train time. I know I was in high spirits earlier and this may seem quite sudden, but it's really not. We've been sitting here for ninety minutes, which is plenty of time to become completely numb, which is what I am. Physically, emotionally, and spiritually numb.

PERRY   I see. Perhaps we'd better leave then.

NINA   Oh Perry, please don't feel you have to leave on my
              account. If you're actually enjoying the performance,
              for some obscure reason, then—

PERRY   But I promised Henry I'd see you to your train. That's
              my one true duty of the evening.

NINA   Not necessary. Look, it's just now half past eight. I'll
              be fine. The fiends aren't out and about till later.

PERRY   Well, you know...I wouldn't mind seeing the dragon. I
              think he's coming up right away.

NINA   Then stay for it. I insist.

PERRY   (*standing*) At least let me see you down to the door.

NINA   (*getting up*) Please, don't feel you need to. There's
              always such a crush of people in the lobby. Come to
              think of it, there'll probably be a bit of a stampede to
              the exit and you might be safer here. (*seeing
              EVELYN's coat*) Is that your coat?

PERRY   No. I checked mine.

NINA   Good for you. It must belong to that mysterious
              woman you saw. I wonder who she is. Perhaps a
              renegade standee. Ah well, at least you'll have
              company, and I don't have to feel like such a heel for
              abandoning you.

PERRY   She may not feel obliged to socialize with me.

NINA   Maybe not. But maybe you'll have a wonderful first
              date. Just think, three and a half hours together and
              only twenty minutes of conversation required. I'll
              scamper away now, and leave you to it.

PERRY   Good night, Nina. It's been a delight.

NINA   Yes, it has, of sorts. And remember at about eleven
              fifteen when Brunhilde awakens from her slumber, that
              I'll be happily entering my own. Good-bye.

PERRY   Good-bye.

> *She goes out. PERRY leans over the edge and looks around. He stretches a bit, then sits down and thumbs through his programme. After a moment, EVELYN enters and sits discreetly in her chair. PERRY hears her and turns.*

Hello.

> *EVELYN looks at him for a second, then nods. PERRY turns back to his programme for a moment, then addresses EVELYN again.*

You know, my friend isn't coming back, so if you'd like, you're welcome to sit up front here. You'd have a better view.

EVELYN   (*after staring at him for a moment*) I understand you.

PERRY   I beg your pardon? I'm sorry, I didn't mean anything untoward. I just thought ... Well, the seat's yours if you want it.

> *He turns away, faintly perplexed. EVELYN gets up abruptly and takes NINA's seat.*

EVELYN   Yes, I will sit in it.

PERRY   Good. I mean, why see less when you can see ... more.

> *EVELYN looks at PERRY, then at the stage, then back at him.*

EVELYN   "Siegfried" is in another language.

PERRY   Yes, it certainly is.

EVELYN   (*letting out a big sigh*) That makes me so happy.

PERRY   It does? Then you must speak German.

EVELYN   No.

PERRY   Oh. (*pause*) Have you seen "Siegfried" before?

EVELYN   I don't know. No.

PERRY   This is my first time as well. I've just been reading the plot synopsis here in the programme. We're going to see a dragon in the next act. Fafner.

                    EVELYN looks at him quizzically.

                 That's the dragon's name. Fafner.

EVELYN   Oh. I see.

                    She looks off rather vacantly. He goes back to his reading.

                 Do you remember meeting me before?

PERRY   Do I? Actually, no. I'm sorry. I don't. I don't think I have. I'm Perry, Perry Spangler.

                    She looks at him intently.

                 Excuse me for asking, but are you foreign?

EVELYN   What?

PERRY   Is English your first language?

EVELYN   Yes.

PERRY   I'm sorry. I guess that's quite a rude question when the answer isn't no.

EVELYN   I have to sit and think for a while. It would be best if we don't talk.

PERRY   I apologize. I should have left you alone. Entirely.

EVELYN   No, no. We can try to talk again later. If there's another ...

PERRY   Intermission?

EVELYN   Yes, that's right. After some more of "Siegfried".

PERRY   Alright. There's another break in about ninety minutes.

EVELYN   Good. I'll talk with you then.

PERRY   I'll look forward to it.

> *They sit for a moment. PERRY gets up.*

EVELYN   Where are you going?

PERRY   Just to the restroom.

EVELYN   The restroom. The men's restroom.

PERRY   That's right.

EVELYN   I went to the women's restroom.

PERRY   Oh? I ... Uh ... Ahhh.

> *He smiles and exits. EVELYN stares ahead thoughtfully as the lights fade.*

Act One, Scene Three

As the music of Act Two of "Siegfried" *concludes and the lights come up. PERRY and EVELYN are applauding enthusiastically.*

PERRY   So ... Did you enjoy that?

EVELYN   Yes I did. Very much. Fafner was frightening.

PERRY   That was an effective bit, wasn't it. But I have to confess, before he came on, there were a few moments when I thought time was standing still.

EVELYN   Yes, I was grateful for that.

PERRY   You were? You know, I'm not sure we're perceiving "Siegfried" on the same level.

EVELYN   I'm just happy when things aren't going too fast, that's all. I can't be rushed. Not tonight.

PERRY   Yes, I think I understand you. It's good then that we're in for at least another eighty minutes at more or less the same tempo.

EVELYN   I'm not sure what to do when it's over.

PERRY   We applaud enthusiastically. We can even holler a bit.

EVELYN   Yes, but after that. I don't know what to do.

PERRY   Well, it'll be close to midnight. I imagine most folks will want to hit the hay.

She looks at him perplexedly.

Go to bed. Go home and go to bed.

EVELYN   So, no one stays on here?

PERRY	I don't think so.
EVELYN	I wonder what I'm going to do. What are you going to do?
PERRY	I'm ... I haven't planned ... Are you asking me out?
EVELYN	What?
PERRY	Should I be ... Should I be asking you to go for a bite to eat after the opera? Is that what's transpiring now?
EVELYN	We could go and get something to eat.
PERRY	Yes, we could. Are we going to? Do you want to?
EVELYN	I'm hungry.
PERRY	Well, alright. We can go to The Automat.
EVELYN	Good. We'll go to The Automat. We'll eat and talk.
PERRY	Talk? About?
EVELYN	"Siegfried".
PERRY	Of course, I don't suppose you'd tell me your name now, would you?
EVELYN	(*turning away*) I have to read the plot synopsis now, for the third act.
PERRY	Sorry. I forgot. You don't want to be rushed.
EVELYN	That's important.

> *She reads intently. PERRY looks ahead. He bites his thumbnail.*

Act One, Scene Four

At The Automat, later that evening. EVELYN sits at a table, watching PERRY remove items from a tray.

PERRY   Here we are. Chicken pot pie and lemonade for you. Cheese blintzes and coffee for me.

EVELYN   These are the items we selected from the automat.

PERRY   Yes. Yes they are.

EVELYN   You've paid for them with nickels and dimes?

PERRY   Right again.

EVELYN   (*after a pause*) Thank you.

PERRY   You're welcome.

               EVELYN looks at him and smiles.

               Hey now, there's a break in the weather.

EVELYN   What?

PERRY   I just saw your first smile of the evening.

EVELYN   Oh. Yes. That's something you noticed. I didn't smile before.

PERRY   It's not something I obsess over particularly, but when I'm out with a girl for the first time ... I guess chicken makes you happy in a way that Wagner never quite could.

EVELYN   (*cutting into her pie*) Chicken pot pie has a crust on top. Inside it has chicken and peas ... and carrots ... and potatoes.

> *She takes a bite and considers.*

I like it. It's delicious.

PERRY
I'm eating cheese blintzes. They have cheese in them. People like these with jam and others like them with mustard. I'm having both because I'm stark raving mad.

> *She stares at him.*

That was a joke. About my being mad. Mustard and jam, that's no joke.

> *She nods. They eat quietly for a moment.*

My name is Perry Spangler.

EVELYN
Yes. You said that before.

PERRY
I wasn't sure you'd remembered.

EVELYN
I did. I remember a number of things. Your name is Perry Spangler. Fafner was the dragon.

PERRY
That's good, two for two. (*pause*) And your name is ...

> *She looks at him, then covers her face with her hands. After a moment, she uncovers it and squints intently.*

EVELYN
You want me to say my name.

PERRY
If it won't compromise you. (*pause*) You could probably even make something up. Just so's I'll have somethin' ta call ya. Please, "My name is..." Do you want me to pick something?

EVELYN
(*foggily*) My name is ... My name is Evelyn Strange.

PERRY
Evelyn Strange? Now you see. I think that's just perfect for you.

EVELYN
My name is Evelyn Strange. I should prove it.

PERRY   That's not necessary, Miss Strange. I want to believe you and so I will.

EVELYN   You should call me Evelyn.

PERRY   I will, if you'll call me Perry.

EVELYN   Perry Spangler. Evelyn Strange. Fafner. Brunhilde.

PERRY   Sounds like the "A" list to me.

EVELYN   Brunhilde knew Siegfried when she woke up. She knew who he was.

PERRY   I think he introduced himself.

EVELYN   But she sang his name like she knew it. (*singing loudly*) "Oh, Siegfried!"

PERRY   Evelyn! Shhh.

EVELYN   It was what she expected to hear, even though they were meeting for the first time and she'd been asleep for twenty years.

PERRY   I think their destinies were intertwined since the dawn of Norse civilization. Or at least since a previous opera.

EVELYN   But she was never uncertain. And she knew who she was too.

PERRY   Is that unusual?

EVELYN   While I watched the opera. I wished that I was Brunhilde.

PERRY   Because of her certainties?

EVELYN   Yes.

PERRY   Forgive me if I'm misreading your train of thought here, but Evelyn, do you not know who you are?

EVELYN   My name is Evelyn Strange and sense has ruled my life in place of passion.

PERRY   Yes, well I've noticed your fondness for clinical observations. But who are you ... specifically?

EVELYN   My name—

PERRY   I know your name, Evelyn. I'm wondering what you do. Actually, I'm wondering if you know what you do. Or if you know where you are. In fact, I'm just wondering what you know. About anything. (*pause*) You may not be able to answer succinctly. I know I wouldn't.

EVELYN   (*after a pause*) I know what's in chicken pot pie. Other than that, Perry Spangler: Fafner. Evelyn Strange.

PERRY   Why did you go to the Metropolitan Opera tonight?

EVELYN   I had a ticket for "Siegfried".

PERRY   Right. Silly question.

EVELYN   In fact I had two tickets. I was walking on Park Avenue and I reached into my pocket and they were there. "Siegfried" at the Metropolitan Opera at seven pm. I walked over at once. What else could I do?

PERRY   Wait a minute. Are you telling me ... Should I understand that before this happened, you don't know where you were?

EVELYN   That's right. I don't.

PERRY   And I guess we mean "before" in pretty much the largest possible way, which is to say that you don't remember what you might have been doing at any previous point in your life.

EVELYN   That's right too.

PERRY   You don't remember what you did this morning or last
               night or last year. You don't remember where you
               grew up or who your parents were.

EVELYN   Please stop. I feel stupid.

PERRY   Well you shouldn't. I don't think you're stupid. I think
               you have amnesia.

EVELYN   I have amnesia.

PERRY   That'd be my guess. You're a little young to have just
               forgotten everything over time, I'd say. You've
               probably suffered a trauma or an injury of some kind
               Does your bead hurt? Have you bumped it on
               anything?

EVELYN   (*touching her head*) I don't think so. My head feels
               fine. I have amnesia.

PERRY   Right. You've lost your memory, except for your
               name. Wait a minute. Have you checked to see if
               you've got any identification in your pockets? Didn't
               you say you could prove your name was Evelyn
               Strange?

EVELYN   (*taking out a small coil notepad*) This is all I have.

PERRY   (*looking at the cover*) Evelyn Strange. (*opening it and
               looks at the first page*) My name is Evelyn Strange.

               *He flips through the remaining pages with
               increasing perplexity.*

               But what the... What's all the rest of this? Is this
               Arabic? All these squiggles...

EVELYN   I don't know.

PERRY   You can't read it?

EVELYN   I stared at it. I looked at every page. It doesn't mean
               anything to me at all.

PERRY   What do you want to bet it's kind of important, huh?
               And this first page, is this your handwriting?

EVELYN   I thought so, I don't know.

PERRY   (*giving her a pen and a napkin*) Here, write on this.
               Just write what it says in the book. (*covering the
               notebook*) But don't copy it.

                    EVELYN writes, then slides the napkin back.

               "My name is Evelyn Strange and sense has ruled my
               life in place of passion." Why that again? That's not
               what it says here?

EVELYN   It isn't?

PERRY   No. But the writing's the same, that's clear. You wrote
               the first page, if not the next hundred. This is
               definitely progress and it'll be fascinating to see this
               mystery unravel. (*He pauses a moment, shrugs, and
               gives back the book*) Here. Don't lose it.

                    *She reaches over to the chair where their coats are
                    draped, and slides it into a pocket.*

EVELYN   So, what do we do next?

PERRY   What do you do next? Go to the police. Then see a
               doctor.

EVELYN   The police? Do you think I've done something wrong?

PERRY   Probably not. But they can tell you if you're missing.
               If someone has reported you missing.

EVELYN   Who would do that?

PERRY   I don't know. Your mother. Your husband.

EVELYN   I'm not married.

PERRY   How can you be sure?

EVELYN   I'm not wearing a ring. I don't think you're married
                because you're not wearing a ring either.

PERRY   Do you always check?

EVELYN   It seems I do.

PERRY   Well that's positive. We've identified one of your
                habits.

EVELYN   Will that help us?

PERRY   In the short term, probably not much.

EVELYN   I check for wedding rings. I have amnesia. I walk on
                Park Avenue. Fafner. Perry. Perry.

PERRY   What?

EVELYN   These are the things I know. I want them to tell me
                my story. My name is Evelyn Strange and sense ...
                sense.

                She lowers her head and sighs.

PERRY   Are you tired, Evelyn?

EVELYN   I'm very tired. I think I'm going to fall asleep.

PERRY   Where are you going to spend the night?

                She looks at him vacantly.

                Do you want me to take you to the police station?

EVELYN   They'll ask me questions.

PERRY   Probably. But they'll take care of you. They might
                have to keep you in a holding cell for the night, but—

EVELYN   A cell? A jail cell?

PERRY   Well, a little like that, or not. Just somewhere you'll
                be safe.

EVELYN   I don't think I should go to jail.

PERRY   But you're not understanding what I—

EVELYN   I DON'T WANT TO GO TO JAIL!!

          She bursts into tears.

PERRY   Alright! Fine! But I don't know what the alternatives
          are. I can't take you home with me. I live in a
          rooming house with other people and it just wouldn't
          be right. Maybe the police would put you in a hotel.
          It's quite possible.

EVELYN   (*after a pause*) I'm sorry I yelled. You should go. It's
          not up to you to look after me.

PERRY   That's right, it's not. But you know, I can't quite see
          my way clear to leaving you in The Automat without
          an identity. I might, if you were just some scruffy
          vagrant, but you're a well-put-together young woman
          who appreciates Wagner, and so I think that if you're a
          little displaced it might be a good idea for me to help
          you, but I'm not sure what to do beyond making
          sensible suggestions involving medicine and the law.

EVELYN   (*after a pause*) Do you have twenty dollars I could
          borrow?

PERRY   What?

EVELYN   (*sighing*) I'm so tired. If you'd loan me some money I
          could just go to a hotel and get some sleep right away.
          If I had to answer more questions right now, I think I'd
          probably just sound more crazy than I already have.
          And you know, I might just wake up in the morning
          and remember everything and then we'd never have to
          trouble anyone else.

PERRY   Would you promise to go to the police, first thing in
          the morning?

EVELYN   Of course. If I wake up and don't know who I am,
          that'll be the first thing that I do.

PERRY	You could be in some sort of danger you know.
EVELYN	(*turning away*) I know. The police will help me.

> *PERRY stares at her sad and beautiful profile for a moment, then takes out his wallet.*

PERRY	This doesn't leave me with much for the weekend.
EVELYN	I'm sorry. If it's trouble for you then I—
PERRY	No, I shouldn't have said that. I'm just going to go in to work anyway.
EVELYN	To work? Of course. You have a job. What is it?
PERRY	I read for a publishing house. I edit.
EVELYN	You're an editor.
PERRY	I edit before the editor does. I'm a sub-editor.
EVELYN	Perry Spangler is a sub-editor.
PERRY	I don't think that's one of the things you need to keep at the forefront of your consciousness.
EVELYN	Will you tell me where you work so I can find you again?
PERRY	(*after a pause*) I suppose.
EVELYN	I'll want to pay you back the money.
PERRY	That's not necessary.
EVELYN	But I want to. And I'll want to tell you who I am once I've found that out. You'll want to know, won't you?
PERRY	Yes. I suppose you could ... write me a letter.
EVELYN	Or I could ... Oh. I understand you.
PERRY	(*handing her a business card*) Here's the address.

EVELYN   "Ferrer and Sons." Are you one of them?

PERRY   The sons? No Evelyn, my name is Spangler.

EVELYN   Of course. And the sons are named Ferrer.

PERRY   Actually, there aren't any sons. My boss is just optimistic.

           EVELYN looks a little perplexed.

      Maybe that's a bit advanced for you at the moment. (*getting up*) Come on. I know of a hotel a few blocks from here. I'll walk you over.

EVELYN   You'll walk me to a hotel.

PERRY   That's right. That's what I said. It's the Livonia and I think it's decent because the coffee shop is up to snuff, I mean respectable. No cracks in the china.

EVELYN   Perry...

PERRY   Yes?

EVELYN   Thank you very much.

PERRY   You're welcome.

           She smiles at him.

      Aha. The second smile of the evening. I knew there was a reason I hadn't fled.

EVELYN   Pardon me?

PERRY   Never mind. Let's go.

EVELYN   Alright.

           They pick up their coats and exit.

Act One, Scene Five

PERRY is at his desk, the following morning.
He's reading a manuscript and making notes on it
with a pencil. After a moment, he takes a cigarette
from a pack on his desk and searches his pockets
for a match. Not finding one, he crosses to the
coat rack where his coat is hanging. He checks the
pockets and is startled to find EVELYN's
notebook in one of them. He holds it and stares at
it for a moment, then retrieves a packet of
matches and returns to his desk. He lights the
cigarette and flips through the book. After a
moment, there is a quick knock and LEWIS
HAKE steps in.

LEWIS   Spangler? What the hell are you doing?

PERRY   (*pushing the notebook aside*) Ah Mr. Hake, won't you
come in? What the hell does it look like I'm doing?

LEWIS   I think you're hard at work on a Saturday morning.

PERRY   There's no use denying it. You've caught me.

LEWIS   Have you done this before?

PERRY   On occasion.

LEWIS   But why? Is it because you're alone in life?

PERRY   That's presumptuous.

LEWIS   What, that you're alone or that that's the reason you're
here?

PERRY   I think it might be more to the point to wonder what
you're doing here.

LEWIS	I forgot my datebook. Now I've collected it and I'm going to leave the office and not return till Monday.
PERRY	You should have just called me. I'd have told you the date.
LEWIS	No doubt, but ... (*opening the book*) what I really wanted were these dry cleaning tags. Now I'll be able to retrieve my shirts.
PERRY	You couldn't have left them till Monday?
LEWIS	I wanted my shirts today, dammit! Today! Today!
PERRY	You're saying you didn't want to wait?
LEWIS	Exactly.
PERRY	Well that's why I'm here too, I wasn't willing to wait a day longer to make my marginal notes on this fine new work of fiction for males aged eight to thirteen. *The Blungren Boys Build A Hide-Out.* Also, I find myself a bit short of cash for the weekend, and this is my practical solution for making it through.
LEWIS	Did you have a reckless Friday night?
PERRY	I wouldn't call it that. I attended "Siegfried" at he Met in the company of the boss's wife.
LEWIS	Come again?
PERRY	Ferrer stuck his head in here late yesterday afternoon, and said he was unable to attend the opera as planned, and would I sit in with the lovely Nina.
LEWIS	Was it at her request?
PERRY	I don't think so. She seemed quite surprised, though she was completely gracious. I should add that she absconded at the earliest possible opportunity.
LEWIS	She left you alone at the Met?

PERRY	Well not completely. There was another young woman seated in our box, and of course a couple of thousand people were lurking above and below.
LEWIS	Ah, another girl in the box? Did you strike up a conversation about things Wagnerian?
PERRY	Sure. It's kind of unavoidable when you're in a confined space with someone and watching "Siegfried".
LEWIS	So what was she like? Blonde? Brunette? Vivacious? Cruel?
PERRY	Those things and more.
LEWIS	Did you take her out afterward?
PERRY	All these questions. What do you want with this information?
LEWIS	Well you see Perry, I was telephoning you repeatedly at home up until at least one o'clock last night. The opera's long but not quite that long.
PERRY	Alright, yes. We went to The Automat.
LEWIS	Ah, I knew it. So, is she a big eater? Will you see her again? Tonight? Will you see her tonight?
PERRY	No. I don't know. Yes. Maybe. Possibly never. You decide. Why were you calling me?
LEWIS	I wasn't. That was an out and out lie.
PERRY	I'm too easy. Sometimes I hate myself.
LEWIS	Don't do that. Just watch your back every hour of every day. So, this Blumgren book, is it in code?
PERRY	What?
LEWIS	(*picking up EVELYN's notebook*) The script is a little unconventional.

PERRY   That's not the Blumgren book. It's something else.

He tries unsuccessfully to snatch the notebook from LEWIS, who darts away and flips to the first page.

LEWIS   "My name is Evelyn Strange." Well I'm hooked. (*flipping through the pages*) Looks like tough sleddin' after that, though. And the explanation is ... ?

PERRY   It's an unsolicited manuscript. From a writer in Khartoum. I have to find a translator and I don't think it'll be easy.

LEWIS   Actually, I think I have seen this kind of script before.

PERRY   Well what is it. Who would be able to read this?

LEWIS   Only a few thousand New Yorkers. Finding the right ones ... that'll be your challenge.

He closes the notebook and puts it on the desk.

Here you are. I'm not intrigued in the least. Remember that. Remember it always.

PERRY   But—

LEWIS   Perry, it's really none of my business.

PERRY   You're right, of course. Are you going to leave soon?

LEWIS   I think that would be appropriate.

There's a knock at the, door and NINA steps in.

NINA   Gentlemen, good morning. May I interrupt?

LEWIS   Mrs. Ferrer, good morning.

NINA   Good morning ... Mr. Hake. Mr. Spangler, you're here, so the opera must have concluded.

PERRY   That's right. It just let out, minutes ago.

LEWIS   Yes, I hear you did "Siegfried" last night.

NINA   I tried, valiantly, but I'm afraid I failed. My little soul was crushed and I had to take it home.

PERRY   So Nina, I take it you made it back to Westchester without incident?

NINA   Not exactly. I was scurrying toward Grand Central when all of a sudden I felt a strange force pulling me off my intended course and drawing me toward the Biltmore Hotel. I was then abruptly sucked in through the revolving door and hurled into a room with a comfortable bed, whereupon I ordered a brandy, drained it at a gulp and fell into a deep and untroubled sleep which ended just over an hour ago.

PERRY   So you haven't been home? Obviously not.

NINA   Oh, I just couldn't, Perry. I couldn't face riding a train all the way to Westchester. Not stupefied as I was.

PERRY   I do hope you called Henry and told him where you were.

NINA   Of course I did. Not that that's really your affair.

PERRY   I'm only concerned since technically I was responsible for you.

NINA   Ah yes, I'm sorry I snapped at you. I failed to consider that your admonitions arose out of self-interest. Rest assured. I called him the moment I checked in.

PERRY   Good. Perfect. I'm out of it.

NINA   Of course he wasn't home yet, so I couldn't really tell him where I was. I called this morning when I awoke, but it was late and I obviously missed him. Now it's occurred to me that he might well be out searching desperately for me, and that's why I've stopped by the office, thinking I might tell him "For God's sake Henry. I'm fine." Have you seen him?

PERRY	Nope.
LEWIS	Not today.
NINA	Well if you do. I hope you'll pass on the message. And now I really must go shopping. I had to make a quick stop at Macy's this morning in order to have suitable day wear, and that's left me tantalized and unfulfilled.
LEWIS	So you'll be heading home this afternoon? In case we're asked?
NINA	I should think so. But you know, I might take in a matinee. I feel a bit gypped after last night.
LEWIS	Right then. A matinee. At around two o'clock?
NINA	I'd say precisely at two o'clock.
LEWIS	Good then. We'll pass that on. Or rather, Mr. Spangler will.
NINA	Now, I'm wondering what exactly you fellows are doing here on a fine Saturday?
LEWIS	Perry's come in to do extra work, and I'm just here to gawk in disbelief.
NINA	Such admirable team work. My husband's a lucky employer. I thank you for your time gentlemen. I'll see you about, I'm sure.
PERRY	Good-bye, Nina.
LEWIS	Good-bye, Mrs. Ferrer. I hope your afternoon is pleasant.
NINA	Thank you. I hope yours is too.

She smiles at them both and exits.

PERRY	Lewis, don't you think you ought to escort her downstairs?

LEWIS	Not necessarily. Why?
PERRY	Because you're a gentleman and she's the charming wife of our boss.
LEWIS	Who was left in your care, not mine.
PERRY	But we know that I'm an unfit guardian. That's neither here nor there because what I really want to say is this. Get out of my office.
LEWIS	Oh, I understand. You're expecting someone?
PERRY	No.
LEWIS	Is it the author from Khartoum? Or a lady. Or a lady author from Khartoum?
PERRY	(*laying his head down*) Wouldn't you rather be somewhere else?
LEWIS	Eventually. I just want to meet this woman.
PERRY	Lewis, there isn't a woman.
LEWIS	That's too bad. It must be downright depressing. You probably shouldn't be alone.
PERRY	It is torture merely to know you.

> *LEWIS cackles and there is a knock at the door.*
> *EVELYN steps in.*

EVELYN	Excuse me ...
LEWIS	Oh my!
EVELYN	I'm looking for Mr. Spangler. Ah. Hello, Perry.
PERRY	Oh. Hello ... there.
LEWIS	Say, I know who you are.
EVELYN	(*gasping*) Do you?

LEWIS Well I don't know your name, but I'm quite certain you're the girl Perry took to The Automat in the middle of last night.

EVELYN You think so? And what if you're wrong?

LEWIS I ... Then I may have embarrassed my friend to a degree that merits little or no forgiveness.

EVELYN That's correct. Fortunately I am that girl.

LEWIS I'm relieved to hear it. My name is Lewis Hake.

EVELYN I'm pleased to make your acquaintance Mr. Hake. My name is ...

She notices PERRY behind LEWIS gesturing frantically for her not to speak and indicating the notepad.

Brunhilde. Brunhilde Madison.

LEWIS Ah yes. Like the avenue below.

EVELYN That's right. Avenues run north and south. Streets run east and west.

LEWIS They certainly do. So Brunhilde, you must have identified very strongly with the heroine of last evening's opera.

EVELYN Yes, very much. I remarked so to Perry at The Automat.

PERRY That's right. It was only because you have the same name though.

EVELYN Yes, Perry. That's evident to us all. Mr. Hake, do you also work here? Are you a sub-editor as well?

LEWIS I am. But unlike Perry, I only read non-fiction and I only do it on weekdays.

PERRY Lewis was just leaving. He's in quite a hurry.

EVELYN   Oh? Where are you off to?

LEWIS   I don't think it matters. It was nice to have met you, Miss Madison.

EVELYN   Please, call me Brunhilde.

LEWIS   Sure, why not. Oh and Perry, I'll take this notepad.

He snatches up the notepad and crosses quickly away from the desk.

I have a friend who can translate it for you in no time.

EVELYN   Isn't ... that ...

PERRY squawks at her surreptitiously.

LEWIS   I'll have it done for Monday.

PERRY   But no, you don't have to do that I'd rather be completely responsible for it ... for whatever reason ...

LEWIS   Don't worry, I'm not going to read it. Not if I discover it's overly personal. Before the end.

He smiles and darts out.

EVELYN   Perry, am I keeping up? He has my notebook, but he doesn't know that it's mine.

PERRY   Right.

EVELYN   Why?

PERRY   He saw it on my desk and immediately suspected me of being involved in some kind of intrigue. I didn't want him to know that you were Evelyn Strange, because I didn't want him to become more curious than he already was. Obviously things haven't worked out well for me.

EVELYN   But is it wrong of him to suspect you're involved in intrigue when in fact you actually are?

PERRY Yes! That's the whole intrigue thing! No one should suspect. But that's really irrelevant. What I want to know is why I happen to be in possession of the notebook.

EVELYN I put it in your coat by accident.

PERRY Oh, of course. And now you haven't been able to go to the police because you're lacking that crucial piece of evidence. Correct?

EVELYN That's right, but—

PERRY And you want to drag me back into this because you think for some reason that'll make it easier for you? Well it won't work because I'm crabby today and I've half a mind to run to the window and scream for the law.

EVELYN I'll be honest with you Perry. I left the book there so I'd have an excuse to come and see you again. You were so nice to me last night and you really didn't have to be. I thought ... Well, obviously I was wrong. But I want you to know that when I first put the pad in your pocket I thought, just for that moment, that your coat was my own.

PERRY But my coat is dark and yours is light.

EVELYN Yes, but I thought otherwise for a second. It was a peculiar certainty and then it went away. And then I decided to leave the pad where it was.

PERRY I see. Are there any other certainties you're concealing from me?

EVELYN No, but I have made another important discovery which I'll share with you, so long as you're interested.

PERRY (*pressing his temples with his hands*) This isn't going to end, is it?

EVELYN Oh come on, you're fascinated by my dilemma.

PERRY   (*taking out a cigarette*) Alright, sure but that doesn't make me remarkable. Please accept that. I must say, you're a little more alert today, a little more in the game.

EVELYN   Getting a good night's rest seems to be the best thing a girl can do for herself, at least in my limited experience. (*as PERRY lights his cigarette*) I guess you smoke.

PERRY   Yeah. Does that surprise you?

EVELYN   Well you didn't last night.

PERRY   I don't smoke socially. Just when I'm at work.

EVELYN   What's that saying? Don't smoke where you work? Don't smoke where you live?

PERRY   Don't sleep where you work.

EVELYN   Don't smoke where you sleep. Don't smoke in bed. That's it! Can I have a cigarette?

PERRY   Do you think you're a smoker?

EVELYN   Don't know for sure. I might be.

> *She takes a cigarette and he lights it for her. She inhales deeply and exhales with confidence.*

PERRY   I guess that answers that question. So...what is the discovery of the day?

EVELYN   Simply this, I do exist and there's proof.

PERRY   Please, go on.

EVELYN   When you left me at the Livonia Hotel, I went in and asked for a room. I said my name was Evelyn Strange and when the clerk went to write it in the register, he found I'd already checked in. And what's more, I'm paid up for the rest of this month and all of the next. I said I was in and out of town so much that I was starting to lose track of simple details, and I asked for a spare key since mine was obviously in my luggage which hadn't yet arrived. He gave it to me and I went up to my room.

PERRY   And what did you find there?

EVELYN   A bed, a bath, and a closet.

PERRY   No personal belongings?

EVELYN   A dressing gown. A pair of slippers. Some lipstick. A Bible. What do you make of all that?

PERRY   Well, obviously you're a devout woman who leads a life of Spartan leisure in mid-town Manhattan.

EVELYN   Don't you think it's at least remarkable that I have a home and that we found it.

PERRY   I'll admit I'm relieved. Shocked too. But mostly relieved. So what are your plans?

EVELYN   I don't know. What are you doing today?

PERRY   You misunderstand me. What are your plans?

EVELYN   Alright, this is what I figure. I probably have a job, most people do. But today is Saturday and tomorrow's Sunday, so I won't be missed at work for another two days. That gives us more time to figure out—

PERRY   Us? No. Stop. Turn. Go. Now. Nix. Uh-uh.

EVELYN   It gives me more time to figure things out. To search for more clues, to prove my own identity. That's within my rights, don't you think?

PERRY   You know what I think.

EVELYN   Well I'm not going to the police now that you've given away my notebook.

PERRY   I think we could get it back without much fuss.

EVELYN	What would be the point? Your friend was going to get it translated. Maybe then the book will tell us all we need to know. Yes? Uh-huh?
PERRY	Alright, that's quite possibly true.
EVELYN	What language is it in anyway?
PERRY	He wouldn't tell me. He just said thousands of New Yorkers speak it.
EVELYN	But which ones? What could it be?
PERRY	My guess is it's a form of Cantonese.
EVELYN	Really?
PERRY	No.
EVELYN	But there is a Chinatown here isn't there? Maybe we should go skulk around.
PERRY	Sure. And if you do speak Cantonese, maybe you can get a job.
EVELYN	That's true. Maybe I should just move on. Think less about the past and more about the future. So, in that vein, shall we have lunch?
PERRY	No thanks. I have work to do. And I can't afford it. I gave away most of the cash I had for the weekend.
EVELYN	I can treat then, since I didn't have to pay for my hotel room. Or maybe I should just give back the cash. Then you'd have to treat, but you might get some change out of it. What do you think?

He stares blankly at her.

Oh. I'm just impossible, aren't I?

She turns away and sighs. He contemplates her beautiful pensive profile then sighs as well.

PERRY   Listen. Keep the money. I'll probably have lunch with you. I just seem to know that without really knowing why. But I do have to work here for another couple of hours.

EVELYN   Alright then, here's what we're going to do. You come and get me at the Livonia. I'm just going to sit in my room and wait for any calls or visits from acquaintances. I think that'll be time well spent.

PERRY   I agree.

EVELYN   I'm in Room 404. Can you remember that?

PERRY   I'll call from the front desk. That'll be more seemly.

EVELYN   Right. Well, I'll be on my way.

PERRY   Good. Thank you. Good-bye.

EVELYN   Perry, you do like me better chipper, don't you?

PERRY   I'll say that I do. But with another night's rest you might be downright dangerous.

EVELYN   And that'd be progress?

PERRY   You'll be able to answer that yourself when the time comes.

EVELYN   Wonderful. Good-bye.

PERRY   Bye.

             She goes out. He looks at his manuscript for a moment, then looks up, considering something. He reaches for a telephone book, looks up a number and dials it.

             Yes, good morning. I'd like to inquire about ticket availability. No no, just in general. I'm interested in the boxes. The lower ones on the Grand Tier.

             The light fades as he talks.

Act One, Scene Six

EVELYN's room in the Livonia Hotel. EVELYN is in her dressing gown, sitting in a chair and reading The Bible. Her dress and coat are draped over another chair. There's a knock at the door and EVELYN crosses.

EVELYN   Yes? Who is it.

VOICE   It's me. The man of the hour.

EVELYN   (*opening the door*) I thought you were going to call from the Oh! Flowers!

              There's a man with a bouquet of flowers covering his face. He lowers it. It's LEWIS.

              Oh! Mr. Hake.

LEWIS   Brunhilde. Hello.

EVELYN   This is a pleasant surprise. Are you coming to lunch?

LEWIS   (*looking about her room*) I beg your pardon?

EVELYN   Not here. We're going for lunch. Perry's invited you?

LEWIS   Yes. Certainly.

EVELYN   Wonderful. He should be here shortly.

LEWIS   Actually, that's a lie.

EVELYN   Well then, what are you doing here?

LEWIS   I've just come to give you these flowers. And this champagne.

              He produces a bottle from behind his back.

EVELYN   Really? Why?

LEWIS   Well I suppose I fell for you the moment I laid eyes on you. I followed you after you left our office.

EVELYN   My goodness.

LEWIS   Perry doesn't know. You mustn't say anything to him or to anyone, and I'm having second thoughts now so I think I'll just go.

EVELYN   Do you want these flowers back? And the champagne?

LEWIS   I don't think so.

EVELYN   You know, Mr. Hake, if you really want to join us for lunch, I could just tell Perry I met you on the street and invited you up.

LEWIS   No. No thank you. I really should go.

EVELYN   Well alright. Thank you for the attention.

LEWIS   Sure. (*turning at the door*) So, are you living here?

EVELYN   Yes. At least until the end of next month. Come by any time.

LEWIS   Wait a minute. You must know ... Are you...

EVELYN   Who? What?

LEWIS   No. Never mind. Is that The Bible?

EVELYN   Verily it is. Have you read the Word of the Lord?

LEWIS   Some bits.

EVELYN   It's unusual, isn't it. I can't really identify with any of the characters, so I don't think I'm getting much out of it. Maybe that's not the point. Anyway, I've been finding it a little tiresome, but now that I've got some champagne to sip—

LEWIS	Who the hell are you?
EVELYN	Me? I ... I'm...
LEWIS	Sorry. Never mind. Gotta go.
EVELYN	(*taking his hand*) Well thank you for your visit, It'll certainly be our secret.
LEWIS	Good.

> *As they clasp hands, NINA pushes the door open gingerly and steps in.*

NINA	Lewis, are you ... Aaa.
LEWIS	(*turning*) What? Oh. Oh-oh.
EVELYN	Good afternoon.
NINA	Lewis? What's going on?
LEWIS	Nothing. Miss Madison and I were just discussing The Bible.
NINA	(*after looking EVELYN up and down*) I don't think that's true.
LEWIS	It seems you two really may not have met. Miss Madison, this is—
NINA	DON'T INTRODUCE US! DON'T SAY MY NAME!
LEWIS	But—
NINA	I have to go right now.

> *She turns and exits.*

EVELYN	That was unpleasant. I'm sorry if it was my fault. Was it?
LEWIS	I've really no idea.

EVELYN	Are you going to go after her?
LEWIS	Yes. Yes I am.
EVELYN	You see now, that just makes sense to me for some reason.
LEWIS	And you won't tell anyone I was here?
EVELYN	Of course not.

> *LEWIS nods and runs out.*

Unless I just lied.

> *She closes the door. She places the flowers on a table and puts the champagne on the floor beside her chair. She sits down and picks up The Bible and finds her place. She pauses and applies lipstick, then begins reading. After a moment, there is a knock at the door.*

Who is it please?

PERRY	It's Perry. Perry Spangler.
EVELYN	(*opening the door*) How many Perry's do you think I know?
PERRY	(*standing in the doorway with a newspaper*) I ...
EVELYN	That's not a real question. Come in. I thought you were going to call from downstairs.
PERRY	I had to see you privately about something that's come up. Oh. You have flowers and champagne.
EVELYN	Yes I do. Good thing, since you've come empty handed.
PERRY	Where did they come from?
EVELYN	The management sent them up. It seems I'm a distinguished visitor.

PERRY	This isn't that sort of hotel. Where did they come from?
EVELYN	If you must know, I bought them myself.
PERRY	With my money?
EVELYN	Am I going to have to account for every cent I spend? If that's so then I don't want your money.
PERRY	Spend it however you like, but when you're through there's not going to be any more.
EVELYN	You think that I can't earn my keep? That I can't take care of myself?
PERRY	Actually Evelyn, I don't doubt that for a minute.
EVELYN	Oh! You think I'm the worst person in the world, don't you?
PERRY	Frankly, I don't know what to think about you anymore.
EVELYN	Did you ever?
PERRY	I was starting to believe I did. But now ... (*holding up the newspaper*) This is today's paper Evelyn. Look here, on the front page.
EVELYN	(*taking the paper*) What? "Body Found in Central Park". That's bad news, but why is it important?
PERRY	Look below, "Police Seek Strange Woman In Connection With Shooting."
	EVELYN looks puzzled and momentarily dismayed.

EVELYN   "The body of an unidentified man was found on a bench near the Central Park Lake early this morning, dead of a single gunshot wound to the head. Covered by a raincoat, the man was initially mistaken by passersby for a sleeping vagrant. Police have suggested robbery as a possible motive for the slaying as the man had no money or valuables on his person. He was also without any form of identification except for an envelope of documents which lay underneath him on the bench. Police have not divulged the contents of these pages, but have announced that they are seeking a woman named Evelyn Strange in connection with the deceased man."

         EVELYN drops the paper and backs away from it.

     It can't be. It can't...

PERRY   Evelyn?

EVELYN   You think I did it, don't you?

PERRY   I don't know. It doesn't say. I think—

EVELYN   You think I murdered that man.

PERRY   No. I—

EVELYN   (*gasping*) I'm on the register here. They'll find me. I've got to get out!

         She runs for the door.

PERRY   Evelyn! Just calm down!

         EVELYN stops at the door. She sighs and turns away from PERRY, showing her beautiful quivering profile.

EVELYN   Just let me go Perry. Just let me go out this door and then you don't have to be involved with this anymore.

PERRY   But I don't think I can. I—

> *EVELYN pulls a small pistol from the pocket of her dressing gown. She turns to PERRY and points it at him.*

EVELYN   Perry, please ...

PERRY   (*backing away*) Evelyn. My God ...

EVELYN   Good-bye Perry. Good-bye forever!

> *She opens the door and darts out, slamming it behind her. PERRY stands still for a moment, then looks around the room. As the final bars of Act One of "Siegfried" play, he takes a deep breath, then snatches up EVELYN's coat, opens the door and runs out, slamming it behind him.*
>
> *Blackout.*
>
> *End of Act One.*

Act Two, Scene One

*A platform at Grand Central Station, a very short
time after the previous scene. The Orchestral
introduction to Act Three of "Siegfried" plays
loudly as NINA strides on carrying her shopping
bags and wearing her sunglasses. She stands
taughtly for a moment, then takes the glasses off
and puts her hand over her eyes. She paces a short
distance from her bags, then returns to them. She
turns from side to side, then sits down on a bench.
She puts her glasses back on as she sees LEWIS
hurrying toward her.*

LEWIS   Nina! Thank God, I've found you.

NINA   Yes, you have. Now leave me alone.

LEWIS   What are you doing here?

NINA   What does it look like I'm doing? I'm waiting for my
train. I'm going back to Westchester to lick my
wounds.

LEWIS   Nina, you don't understand. What you saw wasn't
wha—

NINA   I don't care what it was. I've decided I want out of the
whole sordid mess.

LEWIS   Sordid? That's a slap in the face.

NINA   Lewis, I'm cheating on my husband. You and I are
having an affair. We meet regularly in a cheap hotel,
where I just saw you pawing a blonde, and now we're
having a fight in Grand Central Station. This is sordid!

LEWIS   (*sitting beside her*) I see what you mean, but if you
just let me expl—

NINA	(*with clenched teeth*) Don't sit beside me!
LEWIS	But—
NINA	People will see us. They'll suspect. Just stand and talk like we're casual acquaintances. And don't raise your voice and don't use your arms.
LEWIS	(*shoving his hands into his coat pockets*) Alright, but promise you won't interrupt me.
NINA	I won't. But if the train comes, I'm going to get on it.
LEWIS	I can be brief. I went to the Livonia and knocked on the door, and I knocked precisely at two. The woman you saw me talking to answered the door. I thought I might have gone to the wrong room, but I checked and I hadn't.
NINA	Well you should have left right away. You should have waited downstairs and warned me.
LEWIS	I wanted to, but you see Nina, I couldn't get away because she was someone I knew.
NINA	Oh, here we go. An old flame? An old fling?
LEWIS	Not at all. I met her this morning at the office. She came in to talk to Perry just after you left.
NINA	What?
LEWIS	Apparently they met at the opera last night. He took her to The Automat.
NINA	Lovely. To think that could have been my fate. Wait a minute ... Was this the woman who snuck into our box and sat behind us?
LEWIS	Probably. You didn't actually see her face?
NINA	No, just her coat, which I thought a bit rough and tumble for a lady on the Grand Tier on a Friday night, even if she had checked it. Alright, so you met her this

morning at the office and next thing you know, she's in the very hotel room where you and I have an understood assignation.

LEWIS That's right.

NINA (*staring straight ahead*) If a train for South America passes, I will catch it.

LEWIS But you wouldn't find out what this is all about.

NINA That would be fine.

They sit for a moment.

Lewis, who knows about us?

LEWIS No one, other than your friend, the woman who lets us use her hotel room.

NINA You never told anyone, not even in a roundabout way.

LEWIS No.

NINA Not Perry?

LEWIS Certainly not. Everyone I work with is quite convinced that I'm seeing a whole array of beauties because I take care to describe my nights out in excruciating detail, omitting only to mention that the dates I'm going on about took place three, four, and five years ago. I also maintain a professed fondness for Vivian the airline hostess who's away more often than she's here, and whose travel itinerary I can rattle off rather easily because it's exactly the same as that of my sister, also an airline hostess. If anyone suspects me of anything, it would have to be because they have a suspicious mind.

NINA So you don't think Henry's ever had any sort of an inkling?

LEWIS   I confess, it did occur to me once. About a month ago, he came into my office and shut the door. He asked me quite bluntly if I'd ever been involved with a married woman.

NINA   My God! What did you do?

LEWIS   I raised an eyebrow and smiled and asked if it was something he was considering. He turned bright red and then quickly explained that he'd been reading a new novel about an extramarital affair. He said that it made the woman's point of view quite clear, but he wasn't sure what was in it for the man. He thought, given my reputation, I might be able to enlighten him.

NINA   What did you say?

LEWIS   I told him there were enough single women in the world to keep me from being tempted into that kind of trouble, and then I thanked him for imagining I had a wild and amoral side to my character.

NINA   Why didn't you tell me any of this?

LEWIS   I didn't want you to worry about it.

NINA   You were afraid I'd break it off, weren't you? That I wouldn't want to see you anymore.

LEWIS   Yes, that's correct. I apologize.

NINA   Thanks. And Henry never mentioned this again?

LEWIS   Not to me. I told him to talk to Spangler. I said he wasn't a very likely Lothario, but that he read a lot of fiction and might have some insights.

NINA   Well there we are. Perry's involved in this. He's up to something. Or maybe ... Henry thinks Perry and I ... Oh Lewis!

LEWIS   What?

NINA   When Perry arrived at the opera last night, he handed
              me a note from Henry. (*taking it from her purse*) What
              do you make of this?

LEWIS   "Sorry it couldn't be me, I'm sure you'll find this
              substitute agreeable." Hm. Indifferent or venomous,
              it's hard to say.

NINA   But the next part...

LEWIS   "I may join you later, but that could be ...
              inconvenient."

NINA   But what's crossed out?

LEWIS   I can't quite ... (*peering at the note*) Messy?

NINA   I may join you later, but that could be messy. You
              see, if he thinks Perry ... My God! Perry Spangler?

LEWIS   Not your type?

NINA   Oh he's alright, it's just a shock to be having an affair
              with someone when it wasn't my idea. But Lewis ...
              What about the girl? Who's the girl?

LEWIS   She introduced herself as Brunhilde Madison.

NINA   And he met her at "Siegfried"? How dumb do they
              think we are?

LEWIS   They? Who's they, specifically?

NINA   All of them. I don't know. We're caught in a trap. My
              husband is suspicious of Perry, but Perry's up to
              something too. We're caught in two traps.

LEWIS   What do you think we should do?

NINA   I don't know. I'm afraid to go home. I don't want to
              see Henry. He'll suspect the worst because I didn't
              come home last night, and for once my behaviour was
              completely blameless. It's just not fair.

LEWIS   I don't suppose you want to go back to the hotel.

NINA   Not if there's some self-styled Valkyrie lurking there
         waiting to pounce. I don't understand how they found
         us. It's such a little and obscure hotel.

LEWIS   Actually, You may want to shoot me dead when I tell
         you this, but I recommended the downstairs coffee
         shop to Perry. I told him they made great Reubens.

NINA   Why?

LEWIS   Because they do! And it seemed like a good alibi, in
         case anyone ever saw me going in or coming out of
         the building.

NINA   (*grinding her teeth*) Perry Spangler. He's trouble. I
         hope he gets in an accident.

LEWIS   Nina, listen to yourself.

NINA   Lewis, everything is falling apart. Please, just throw
         me onto the tracks.

LEWIS   That's premature. I think you should just check into
         another hotel while we try to figure things out.

NINA   I can't do that. I can't be alone or I'll go mad. Look at
         me. Doesn't that seem likely?

LEWIS   It sure does, but I don't know what to suggest. You
         don't want to go home. We can't go to my apartment.

NINA   Why not?

LEWIS   It might look rather incriminating, and it's awfully
         close to the office. We could be seen.

NINA   Oh, who cares. We're guilty as hell and everyone's
         going to know it in about five minutes. Take me
         home Lewis. (*clutching his lapels*) Take me home or
         I'll go wild right here in Grand Central.

LEWIS   Alright, fine. If that's what you want. I'm more than
               agreeable. But just calm down. People are looking at
               us.

NINA   Oh no. Oh no. We've got to get out of here.

                    She begins gathering up her shopping bags.

LEWIS   It's probably best if we go separately. You should get
               a cab and I'll take the subway.

NINA   But I'll get there first and then I'd have to wait outside.

LEWIS   Well then—

NINA   I'm not taking the subway! (*screechily*) Not with all
               those crazy people!

LEWIS   I'm just trying to keep things discreet.

                    She grabs him and kisses him hotly.

NINA   There. Now it's too late.

LEWIS   Right. Let's get a taxi.

                    They collect all the bags and flee.

Act Two, Scene Two

> *A back alley, around the same time as the previous scene. EVELYN runs on with PERRY still in hot pursuit. She's still in the dressing gown. He's carrying her coat.*

PERRY   Evelyn, please. Please stop!

EVELYN   No! No. leave me! Get away!

> *He corners her against a wall beside a garbage can.*

PERRY   Evelyn—

EVELYN   (*putting her hand in her pocket*) Now why would you corner me when you know I've got a gun?

PERRY   I guess I'm giving you the benefit of the doubt.

EVELYN   You are? Oh Perry, that's so sweet.

PERRY   (*stepping forward*) Now please ...

EVELYN   Don't come any closer or I'll start screaming.

PERRY   Who for? The cops?

EVELYN   What do you want? Why can't you just leave me alone? Just let me go!

PERRY   Oh for God's sake, why didn't you let me go? You dragged me into this. You planted evidence in my coat.

EVELYN   I didn't know it was evidence. I didn't know I was a criminal. I'm not a criminal! Stop accusing me of that.

PERRY   I haven't accused you once.

EVELYN	Well you hardly have to.
PERRY	You're not being fair, Evelyn.
EVELYN	Fair? Look at the hand I've been dealt.
PERRY	There was nothing in that newspaper story that even suggested you were suspected of the killing. They just want to question you.
EVELYN	Well that's where it starts, isn't it.
PERRY	Not necessarily. You might have some information that they—
EVELYN	Information? I have amnesia! My help they don't need. And how do I deny anything that they accuse me of?
PERRY	But they aren't going to—
EVELYN	Yes they are. I have a gun!
PERRY	You certainly do. How long have you had it?
EVELYN	As long as I can remember. It was in my coat pocket along with the opera tickets.
PERRY	Why didn't you mention this before? Last night ... This morning ...
EVELYN	I was afraid it wouldn't be ... what's that ... seemly?
PERRY	Well you were right, and it doesn't look good. But more than ever I think that turning yourself in would be the best way to find out who you are.

> *EVELYN catches her breath and turns away slightly. She looks at the ground.*

EVELYN	I'm not sure I want to know anymore.
PERRY	Funny, I think I'm starting to feel just the opposite.
EVELYN	(*sharply*) Perry, that's so selfish.

PERRY	It can't be helped. In fact, I've started to formulate a few theories of my own.
EVELYN	Anything you can share with me?
PERRY	Not quite yet. I have to walk around, keep moving. Forward motion helps me think.
EVELYN	Can I come with you?
PERRY	I'm not sure it's a good idea, now that you're a wanted woman.
EVELYN	Then I have to go somewhere and hide till we have some answers. I can't turn myself in, not until I know who I am. Don't you see? These may be the hands that held the gun that put a bullet in that man's head, but right now, I'm not the girl who pulled the trigger. I can't take the rap for her. That wouldn't be justice. Tell me you understand, Perry.

She looks at him pleadingly, quiveringly.

PERRY	Evelyn, it's crazy, but I do.
EVELYN	I'm so grateful for that.

Standing very close, they stare at one another for a moment. He moves forward and they kiss, then he pulls back abruptly.

PERRY	What am I doing? You have no identity!
EVELYN	Is that so bad?
PERRY	For me, yes. That shouldn't have happened. I apologize.
EVELYN	That's not necessary. Not now at any rate. Maybe later I'll feel differently.
PERRY	So ... what's next? Where'll we go? I'm not asking you. I'm just wondering aloud.

EVELYN   Your friend Mr. Hake has my notebook. We should get it from him and have it translated immediately.

PERRY   Yes, you might be right. (*gasping*) Evelyn, your name is in it.

EVELYN   All the more reason to get it back.

PERRY   We'd better go to his apartment.

EVELYN   He might not be there.

PERRY   That's true, but why do you mention it?

EVELYN   Well, I wasn't supposed to say anything, but circumstances have changed. Lewis was in my hotel room just before you arrived.

PERRY   What?

EVELYN   He brought the flowers and champagne.

PERRY   Why?

EVELYN   Well, Perry, you figure it out.

PERRY   That's unbelievably crass. I'd say I was shocked, but then I'd look naive.

EVELYN   Oh go ahead. Wouldn't bother me.

PERRY   How did he know you were there?

EVELYN   At first he said you'd told him. Then he admitted he'd followed me. He was pretty squirrely. I think I really got him going. Oh ... And then a woman came to the door. She seemed to have followed him and she was very upset to see us together.

PERRY   I can't believe you didn't tell me any of this.

EVELYN   Well maybe if you hadn't accused me of murder the minute you walked in the door.

PERRY   Hey! That's not ... Let's just go see Lewis, shall we?

EVELYN   Yes let's. Is that coat for me?

PERRY   Oh. Yes.

EVELYN   Thanks. It was thoughtful of you to bring it.

> *She puts it on over her dressing gown and looks down in dismay at the dangling hem.*

Don't I look stylish. I might just as well run down Broadway screaming "Haul me in! I'm deranged!"

PERRY   Well I'm sorry it couldn't be perfect.

EVELYN   Oh shush. Just turn your back.

PERRY   What?

EVELYN   Look over there!

PERRY   Where?

> *He turns away. EVELYN quickly removes the dressing gown and puts the coat on over her slip.*

EVELYN   (*tossing the dressing gown into the garbage*) There. That's better.

PERRY   Aren't you forgetting something?

EVELYN   Hm? Oh... Ha-ha.

> *She retrieves the dressing gown and takes the gun from the pocket.*

Would you like to carry this?

PERRY   Not even a little.

EVELYN   (*putting it in her pocket*) Alright. Let's go.

PERRY   Yes. Which way?

EVELYN   I think that's up to you.

PERRY   Yes. Yes it is.

He grabs her hand and they hurry away.

Act Two, Scene Three

*LEWIS HAKE'S apartment, later that afternoon.
Various articles of the clothing worn by LEWIS
and NINA in the previous scene are strewn about.
LEWIS enters from the bedroom. He is wearing a
pair of pyjamas and is in the process of buttoning
the tops. He gathers up some of the discarded
clothing and lays it neatly aside. NINA comes out
of the bedroom, artfully draped in a bedsheet.*

NINA   Lewis? What possible reason would you have for
                leaving me alone in the bedroom? What are you doing?

LEWIS   'Tidy as you go, and it never gets to be a big job'.

NINA   Darling, it's too late for that. A hurricane has touched
                down and picking up your trousers is an empty gesture
                at best.

LEWIS   I'm afraid they'll wrinkle.

NINA   Drop them I say. Drop them and come to me.

LEWIS   (*dropping trousers*) Alright.

                *He crosses and they lock in a torrid kiss. When
                they finally break apart, she leans her head on his
                shoulder.*

NINA   Oh Lewis, tell me we can just stay here.

LEWIS   I think we can. I've no plans.

NINA   No, I mean... indefinitely.

LEWIS   I pay my rent so we won't be evicted. Are you saying
                you want to move in?

NINA   No, Lewis. All I really meant was that I wanted to prolong this passionate carnal interlude in order to stave off the mundane intrusions of the outside world.

LEWIS   Ah. I see. I apologize for my literal-mindedness. I'm afraid I've shattered the mood.

NINA   Do you think so?

      She kisses him.

LEWIS   Perhaps not.

NINA   This is a pretty swift pair of pyjamas you're wearing. I hope they were a gift from a family member.

LEWIS   You know, I bought them myself.

NINA   That's pathetic, but it's a relief as well. So, were they a good price? How much?

LEWIS   Why? Are you in the market for pyjamas? For your husband?

NINA   No. Not for him. For myself actually. Wearing a pair of men's pyjamas is something I've never actually experienced.

LEWIS   Maybe you can try these on before too long.

      NINA gives an ecstatic little shiver.

LEWIS   What was that?

NINA   Ya sent me.

LEWIS   Ah. You know, I like what you're wearing too.

NINA   Do you? I'm tired of it. I want to put it back but I don't remember where I got it. Will you show me?

LEWIS   Certainly. In just a minute.

> *He picks up his jacket and rummages in the pockets.*

NINA What are you doing? What is there that's more important than me?

LEWIS Well, I'll tell you Nina, this is something you may find intriguing and provocative.

NINA I hate that sort of thing. Get to the point.

LEWIS Well Nina, on occasion you've alluded to your humble origins in the steno pool.

NINA Yes, but I haven't discussed it in any detail because to do so would be distasteful to me.

LEWIS Nonetheless, you are experienced in the fields of typing and dictation?

NINA (*smiling fixedly*) Lewis, I'm naked and I'm not at home. Humiliation is inches away. What are you doing to me?

LEWIS I need your help Nina, in a clerical matter.

NINA Religious?

LEWIS Uh-uh. (*taking out EVELYN's manuscript and opening it to a page in the middle*) I have here a manuscript written in a language I don't understand. Can you read it?

NINA (*looking at it*) No, certainly n— Oh. Wait. Is this in shorthand?

LEWIS I think it is.

NINA Oh, well then, let's see..."It has ... rained steadily ... for two days." It takes a little effort when it's not your own writing, but yes, I can read this.

LEWIS Hooray! Let's have more.

NINA   "For the first time ... in my life bad weather doesn't
              seem to oppress me. I think only of his arms, his face,
              his back. The look of him, the smell of him as he..."
              Lewis, what is this?

LEWIS   It's a manuscript. Is it all as spicy as that?

NINA   (*flipping back to the first page*) Who wrote this? "My
              name is Evelyn Strange..." (*perusing the first few
              pages quickly*) Where did you come across something
              like this? Whose writing is this?

LEWIS   I assume it's Evelyn Strange's writing, whoever she
              may be. It was on Perry's desk this morning and he
              didn't seem to know a whole lot about it.

NINA   Perry Spangler! Ahhh!

              She flings down the book.

LEWIS   Nina, what is it? What's wrong?

NINA   Perry. I just remembered how much I hate him. He's
              out to get us, right? We know that.

LEWIS   I'm not sure. I've tried not to think about it. But this
              notebook... Is there something in it that you—

NINA   I've no idea what it's all about.

              She stares ahead stonily.

LEWIS   Nina I'm sorry. I didn't mean to upset you all over
              again.

NINA   It's alright. I'll be fine. Lewis, I think I'm going to
              have a bath. A little soak will help me to calm down,
              and while the water's running I'll peruse this torrid
              little text. Then later, when I'm all fresh and clean, we
              can adjourn to the other room where we can recline
              while I read aloud of Strange Evelyn as though I were
              Scheherezade of old, Yes? Yes, yes?

              He shivers ecstatically.

NINA   (*picking up the notebook*) Good then, I'll see you
                soon.

LEWIS   It's such a lie, isn't it. To prolong this?

NINA   Sure. But we're having an afternoon of lies and thank
                God for it. Who knows when we'll get another?

                > *She exits into the bathroom. LEWIS finishes*
                > *picking up the discarded clothing and puts it out*
                > *of the way. The water is heard running in the*
                > *bathroom. LEWIS picks up a newspaper from a*
                > *side table and looks it over. He spots an article of*
                > *interest and peruses it. He is startled and visibly*
                > *shaken by the last line and contemplates it,*
                > *squinting in perplexity. He turns to approach the*
                > *bathroom when there is a knock at the door.*
                > *LEWIS stands frozen in panic. There is a harder*
                > *knock and he approaches the door.*

LEWIS   (*hoarsely*) Who is it? Who's there?

PERRY   Lewis, it's Perry. Perry Spangler.

LEWIS   What do you want?

PERRY   I want to come in, Lewis. I have to talk to you.

LEWIS   Could you come back later? I'm resting.

PERRY   It's urgent, Lewis. I'm in a bit of trouble.

LEWIS   What kind of trouble?

PERRY   I can't explain through the door. Please let me in.

LEWIS   I'm sorry, Perry, but I really can't help you right now.
                I'm just too tired.

PERRY   (*pounding on the door*) Let me in right now, Lewis, or
                I'll kick the door down.

                > *LEWIS opens the door. PERRY pushes his way*
                > *in. EVELYN stands in the doorway.*

LEWIS	For God's sake, Spangler, keep your voice down or I'll be thrown out on my ear.
PERRY	Too tired? Too tired! What the hell kind of friend are you?
EVELYN	Perry, he is in his pyjamas.
LEWIS	Miss Madison. Thank you for the vote of confidence.
EVELYN	You're welcome. Can I have something to drink?
LEWIS	No.
EVELYN	But I'm really thirsty.

> *She passes him and crosses to a sideboard with decanters and glasses on it.*

(*picking up a decanter*) What's this?

LEWIS	It's whisky. Irish whisky. If you're thirsty, I doubt it's what you want.
EVELYN	I'd like to try it anyway. (*pouring a small amount*) It might be something I like.
LEWIS	Perry, get her out of my home.
PERRY	First tell me what you were doing in her hotel room.
LEWIS	I don't know what you're talking about. I've never seen this woman before in my life.
PERRY	You met in my office just hours ago ... and that's even beside the point. I know you were at the Livonia today.
LEWIS	(*to EVELYN*) You said you weren't going to tell.
EVELYN	I must have lied. (*sipping whisky*) Whew! Strong stuff.
PERRY	Were you expecting to find someone else in the room?

LEWIS   Yes, I was. That's all I'm going to say.

EVELYN   Was it the woman who showed up while we were
                   talking?

LEWIS   Alright, yes. And that's really all I'm going to say.

PERRY   Can you just tell us her name?

LEWIS   No. This is really none of your business. I know it for
                   a fact.

PERRY   Oh, that's so stupid. How could you know it?

LEWIS   (*slapping at PERRY*) Spangler, just get out of here!
                   Just get out, the both of you.

EVELYN   I'm not finished my whisky.

LEWIS   I don't care.

EVELYN   Well you're a lot less pleasant as the day wears on,
                   aren't you? Do you have any cigarettes?

LEWIS   No. I don't smoke.

EVELYN   Really? I sure do. I'm really good at it too. Oh well,
                   maybe I'll just top up my drink then.

PERRY   Evelyn, maybe you shouldn't.

LEWIS   Oh. Hey. Do you mean to say her name's not really
                   Brunhilde?

EVELYN   Surprise!

LEWIS   Wait a minute! Your name is Evelyn? Evelyn what?

EVELYN   My name is Evelyn Strange.

                   She throws back the rest of her whisky.

PERRY   Oh no.

LEWIS	I see. Like the murderess?
EVELYN	What?
PERRY	He knows.
EVELYN	What do you know?
LEWIS	Just what was in the paper. This woman is wanted in connection with a brutal homicide.
EVELYN	I didn't do it!
PERRY	We don't think that she—
LEWIS	Whatever you say. I suppose I ought to call the police, but you'd probably rush me and kill me, so why don't I just let you go quietly and you two can continue your crime spree elsewhere.
EVELYN	You have my notebook. I need it back.
LEWIS	I don't know where I put it.
PERRY	Well why don't we look for it?
LEWIS	I don't think it's here. It's not here. I left it with a friend.
PERRY	We have to find that notebook. It'll have proof of Evelyn's innocence.
EVELYN	That's right. Or my guilt.
LEWIS	Huh?
EVELYN	Lewis, are you running the bathtub?
LEWIS	Yes. What of it?
EVELYN	Don't you think you should go check to see that it's not overflowing?

LEWIS   I suppose I should. But I'm not going to leave you two here to rip up my home in a futile search while I'm out of the room.

EVELYN   But I'm worried. What if there's a flood. Think of your downstairs neighbours.

PERRY   Evelyn's right. You should turn off the water. We could all go do it as a group.

LEWIS   NO!

PERRY   No?

LEWIS   That really won't be—

   In the bathroom, NINA shuts off the water.

PERRY   What the...

EVELYN   Is there...

   LEWIS covers his whole face with one hand and twists it.

NINA   (*offstage*) Oh-oh. Oh no!

   Everyone stands very still. NINA steps out of the bathroom wearing a dressing gown of LEWIS' and holding something behind her back.

   Lewis, I'm terribly sorry. You won't believe what I accidentally went and ... did.

   Seeing the others, she stands transfixed with horror. There is a lengthy pause.

LEWIS   Nina, I'm sorry

PERRY   Mrs. Ferrer ... what ...

NINA   What am I doing here? I'm drawing a bath. And I suppose you may draw your own conclusions.

EVELYN   Mrs. Ferrer? As in...

NINA   Henry Ferrer? That's right. I'm the boss's wife. And I
              wonder who exactly you are, not that I care to make
              your acquaintance.

EVELYN   My name is Evelyn Strange.

              *NINA bites her lip and stares at EVELYN for a
              very long time.*

NINA   I see. And sense has ruled your life in place of
              passion?

EVELYN   Yes, that's right. That's what I believe.

NINA   Well then, Evelyn, this must belong to you.

              *She hurls the notebook at EVELYN's feet. It is
              soaking wet and the ink has run.*

EVELYN   (*with a shriek*) My notebook! It's all wet! The ink's
              run all over the place. It's destroyed! Perry, my
              notebook is completely destroyed.

NINA   So sorry. I'm afraid I dropped it in the bath.

EVELYN   My notebook. Now I'll never know who I am.

NINA   And if you run along right now, I'll never know who
              you are either.

PERRY   Nina! That's just cruel.

NINA   Forgive me for being a little testy. I wonder what you
              were expecting when you set out to ensnare me and
              embarrass me.

PERRY   I didn't. I'm only here for Evelyn's sake.

NINA   Evelyn? For God's sake, stop calling her that.

EVELYN   But it's my name.

NINA turns away with an angry snort.

LEWIS   Nina?

PERRY   Do you know something we don't?

NINA   I only ... Well, who ever heard of a name like that?

PERRY   It's a bit deluxe I'll admit, but it's really all we've got to call her.

NINA   (*utterly perplexed*) Huh?

PERRY   Evelyn has amnesia. The only clue she had to her identity was the notebook that you destroyed. We're certain that there was some clue to her past buried in that peculiar code.

NINA   Well, take my word for it, there wasn't.

PERRY   You read it? You understand that language?

NINA   Perfectly. I learned it at business college.

PERRY   What? It's...

LEWIS   It's shorthand, Perry. Standard secretarial shorthand.

PERRY   Really?

EVELYN   I know shorthand?

NINA   Lucky you. It's quite a marketable skill.

LEWIS   Nina is a former dicta-typist.

PERRY   Really?

NINA   (*after casting a glare at LEWIS*) Yes, really. But beyond that, I didn't just read what was in that notebook. I also wrote it.

PERRY   What?

LEWIS   No!

EVELYN   How?

NINA   I don't think I've much dignity left to lose, at least among we four friends, so I will confess simply that I am Evelyn Strange.

LEWIS   Nina! Oh, no. No. No.

NINA   It's the name I registered under at the Livonia, where Lewis and I had our afternoon trysts. He never knew it, and in fact thought I borrowed the room from a friend. We shared one important secret and I thought it best not to have smaller ones as well. I have also kept a diary in which I've written every detail of our affair. That's what's in the notebook and had any of you read it. I'm sure you'd have found it shocking and mildly pornographic. But you see ... Miss ... it wouldn't have told you anything about yourself. I happily take credit for it now, for it's the chronicle of what has been a beautiful and transforming experience in my life. There, I've said it all. I'm Evelyn Strange, and I don't care who knows it.

LEWIS   (*handing NINA the newspaper*) Nina, I think you'd better have a look at this before you say anything more.

NINA   What? What's this? You want me to read the paper?

LEWIS   Just this article here.

                  NINA snatches the paper and reads the article quickly. When she's done, she throws the paper down with a cry.

NINA   I don't know anything about this. It has nothing to do with me. Lewis, how long have you known about this? Why didn't you say anything?

LEWIS   I've only known for a few minutes. Things have been a little chaotic here, and up until seconds ago. I thought this would have involved her, not you. Her!

NINA
Well it doesn't involve me. I haven't been anywhere near Central Park for weeks. I'm Nina Ferrer for God's sake. If she's going to go around pretending to be Evelyn Strange, then I think there's no reason to let her off the hook in this instance.

EVELYN
I'm not pretending!

NINA
Fine. All the better for me.

LEWIS
I'm just wondering about the diary. If that's a transcription, where's the real one?

NINA
At home, in a safe and private place.

LEWIS
Where?

NINA
I beg your pardon?

LEWIS
Is there ... Is there much about me in it?

NINA
Well yes, I'd say there's a little something on every page.

LEWIS
My name?

NINA
No, that mattered less than other things. I refer to the fact that you are someone my husband sees from time to time, but any other descriptions wouldn't likely lead to your being recognized under any but the most intimate circumstances. Now, I realize there are still unanswered questions, but my bath water is getting cold, so I must ask to be excused.

She turns to go.

PERRY
Nina, please ... There's just one more thing we really think you ought to know.

NINA
I DON'T WANT TO KNOW ANYTHING ELSE!!! I've confessed my crime! I'm an adulteress and the whole world's about to know it, but that's as far as I go in any of this. I'm not involved in the rest of your

	intrigues and I've nothing to do with this woman, whoever she may be!
EVELYN	Mrs. Ferrer ... please ... Let Perry speak. You need to know this.
NINA	(*after a moment*) You can tell me one more thing. Perry. Just one more.
PERRY	Nina, I'm sorry, but I think, we think ... the man in the park ... the murdered man ... We think it's Henry.
NINA	Henry? My husband?
LEWIS	Perry, why?
PERRY	He wasn't home last night when you called. I've been telephoning him all day and there's still no answer. What's more, Nina, he never called me to find out why you didn't come home from the opera. He hasn't shown up at the office either.
LEWIS	But that's hardly sufficient reason to—
PERRY	The memory loss suffered by Evelyn, this Evelyn, could have been induced by exposure to some horrific event, something she witnessed or discovered or participated in. Something like a murder. Completely disoriented following this terrible experience, Evelyn found tickets to "Siegfried" in her coat pocket and so she made her way to the Metropolitan Opera because she had no idea what else to do. I've checked the status of these particular tickets, and the only person she could have got them from was the subscriber who held the box for the season. You can't buy two tickets in a box, you have to buy all four, and the subscriber with these four seats was Henry Ferrer.

He looks at the others. They all sit in silence.

PERRY   The envelope found underneath the dead man connects
             him with one Evelyn Strange. Her diary, or a facsimile
             of it, was found in the possession of this lady, who
             was also the custodian of Henry Ferrer's spare opera
             tickets. That's as much as I knew when we came here,
             but now we know that there's another Evelyn Strange
             and she is in fact Mrs. Henry Ferrer. (*pause*) I think
             that's everything. I'm sorry, Nina. I know it's all
             circumstantial, but I can't help believing I'm right
             about this.

NINA   (*after a long silence, turning to EVELYN*) You're
             wearing my husband's raincoat.

EVELYN   I am?

LEWIS   Nina, are you sure?

NINA   Yes, I am. I bought it for him. I saw that coat at the
             opera last night. I knew there was a reason it bothered
             me. I really don't like that coat.

LEWIS   Then why...

NINA   Why did I buy it for him? I don't like my husband
             either, Lewis. It might seem tasteless to bring that up
             at this particular moment, but I'm really just trying to
             keep my head on straight right now, and I can't do that
             if I have to make pretences of any kind.

EVELYN   I'm sorry if the coat bothers you, I'd take it off but I'm
             not quite dressed underneath.

NINA   No? I suppose I'm in a similar pickle. You know, I've
             been shopping all day and I must have something
             suitable for you.

EVELYN   Really?

NINA   Why not? Just come into the bedroom.

EVELYN   In there?

LEWIS   Maybe that's not—

PERRY	Evelyn, don't!
NINA	Well, I guess I know exactly what you all think of me.
PERRY	I'm sorry.
LEWIS	I wasn't ... I just ...
NINA	I've no concealed weapons. Do I have to prove it? (*pause*) Gentlemen?
EVELYN	That won't be necessary. Let's go.

They exit into the bedroom.

LEWIS	You know, they're a frighteningly cool pair. Do you think one of them did it? Do you think they're in on it together?
PERRY	Did it? In on it? What is it exactly?
LEWIS	The murder. The plot.
PERRY	One might suspect so. Lewis, what were you doing last night?
LEWIS	Nothing. Nothing in particular. I was at home, and I suppose I was out for a bit. I went to the corner store.
PERRY	At about what time?
LEWIS	What time? I don't know. Seven thirty. Eight.
PERRY	I wonder why Henry didn't offer you his ticket. He didn't, did he?
LEWIS	No. I'm sure he assumed I was busy. I may have told him that Vivian was coming into town for the weekend.
PERRY	But she didn't?

LEWIS	Well no. Perry, I might as well tell you now ... Vivian doesn't actually exist.
PERRY	I see. (*pause*) So there are no witnesses to your actual whereabouts and you in fact created an alibi that was an out and out lie?
LEWIS	Yes, I suppose, but—
PERRY	You were also in the office relatively early on a Saturday morning. Not at all characteristic.
LEWIS	I told you. My shirts ...
PERRY	Where are they?
LEWIS	I didn't get them. Things came up. You know that. Are you saying ... You think I murdered Henry?
PERRY	Someone must have. Someone with opportunity, which we've established for you, and motive—
LEWIS	Motive?
PERRY	Yes. There's always a motive, when someone kills their boss, or say, the husband of their mistress ... I won't speculate on what drives you particularly, Lewis, because frankly, you've become a bit of a stranger to me today. I'm sure though, that if you look into your own heart, you can find something sufficiently nasty.
LEWIS	I don't know why you're picking on me.
PERRY	I'm not picking on you. I'm just speculating on reasons you might be accused of murder.
LEWIS	Well, what about you? You were out with the victim's wife last night. You had Evelyn Strange's diary sitting on your desk. You're pretty thoroughly tangled up with the unknown woman who seems to have been the last person to see him alive.
PERRY	There you go. It's tempting to conjecture, isn't it?

LEWIS   Perry, I didn't do it! I didn't murder anyone or steal anyone's diary. A love affair, that's all I'm involved in. A CLANDESTINE LOVE AFFAIR!!

PERRY   Love? Has it gone that far?

LEWIS   You heard Nina. She called it a beautiful and transforming experience. She's chronicled the whole thing in exhaustive detail.

PERRY   I was really wondering about it more from your point of view.

LEWIS   What? Do I love her? Look at the risks I've taken.

PERRY   Yes, you've been downright uncompromising when it comes to lying and cheating and deceiving your friends.

LEWIS   We had to do that. Nina stands to lose a lot. Money, social standing...

PERRY   Things may be different now.

LEWIS   Yes they may. She'll be free and maybe we can think about—

PERRY   Lewis, I'd suggest you have a lawyer present if you're planning to say anything more to anyone, ever.

LEWIS   I'm just trying to say how much I love her. How genuine my feelings are and how honourable my intentions are.

          NINA enters from the bed room in an elegant tea dress.

          Nina please, let me tell you I love you! I want to declare our love in front of other people.

NINA	I can't imagine why you think that would be appropriate at this particular moment, Lewis. For one thing, I may be in mourning. For another, your protestations might be just enough to ensure that we all hang.
LEWIS	But we haven't done anything wrong, have we?
NINA	Haven't we?
LEWIS	What? Are you saying you think I ... Or that—
NINA	I'm not saying anything. (*handing him the dressing gown she wore previously*) Put on your dressing gown Lewis. You have guests.

> *LEWIS puts on the dressing gown. He stands aside, puzzled and miffed.*

NINA	Perry, I place myself in your hands. Tell me what I ought to do.
PERRY	It's really quite simple. Call the police. Tell them what you know.
NINA	I'm not going to do that. What a ridiculous suggestion. Turn myself in? No thank you.
PERRY	You wouldn't be turning yourself in, just by reporting—
NINA	Oh wouldn't I? Perry, I don't want anyone to know I'm Evelyn Strange, but I don't want to lie either. I don't want to come forward and volunteer highly personal information if it might later prove irrelevant.
PERRY	I see. Then Nina, I place myself in your hands. Just tell me what I ought to do.
NINA	I want to know that my husband is dead before I say anything that might embarrass me publicly.
PERRY	Then you want me to identify him?

NINA	I don't see how you could do that without involving the rest of us.
PERRY	Well what do I do then?
NINA	Just what you've been doing all day. Find out more things.
PERRY	Things?
NINA	Find out who that woman is. She knows the truth.
PERRY	And the truth doesn't involve you?
NINA	That'd be what I'm hoping.
PERRY	And what if I just refuse to have anything more to do with any of this?
NINA	Your conscience will eat away at you and your girlfriend will never have a name. But maybe you can live with these things.
PERRY	I don't get it. Last night at the opera, you seemed like such a nice person.
NINA	Really? Even when I walked out in a fit of intolerance?
	They stare at each other for a moment. EVELYN comes out of the bedroom in an attractive skirt and blouse.
LEWIS	Evelyn! That's a very becoming outfit on you.
EVELYN	Thank you, Mr. Hake, but I must ask that you not call me by that name anymore. I know it isn't mine.
NINA	You might as well use it, as long as you're wearing my clothes.
EVELYN	Thank you, Nina, but that wouldn't bring me any closer to discovering my true identity.
NINA	In the meantime, what then? "Hey you"?

PERRY	I'd suggest "Miss Strange" as an apt and helpful compromise.
EVELYN	I guess that'll do. Thank you, Perry.
PERRY	My pleasure, Miss Strange.
EVELYN	So, have we arrived at any further conclusions? Have we determined a plan of action?
LEWIS	Backbiting and recrimination seem to be the order of the day.
EVELYN	Oh? That's not very helpful, is it?
NINA	No, Miss Strange, not very, but it keeps us feisty and loquacious for the challenges ahead.
EVELYN	Pardon me?
PERRY	I'm going to do something decisive. I'm going to leave.
LEWIS	A stopgap at best, Spangler.
PERRY	Not at all, I'm just going to zip around the corner to the offices of Ferrer and Sons. I'll go through the papers on Henry's desk and in his wastebasket and I'll check his calendars and schedules and I'll find out just what he's been up to lately. A good idea, yes?
	The others murmur supportively, then speak in unison.
ALL	I'll come with you.
PERRY	No, I'm going alone. You ladies ought not to be out and about because collectively, you're a fugitive from justice. And Lewis, you are their host.
EVELYN	Are you going to come back?
PERRY	I generally do, Miss Strange.

EVELYN   That's true and I appreciate it.

NINA   I'd like to thank you too Perry, for not turning me in yet.

EVELYN   Turning her in? Did I miss something? Is she guilty?

NINA   (*crossing to the sideboard*) I have to drink now.

LEWIS   Perry, is there anything you'd like us to do while you're gone?

PERRY   Why don't you all just sit quietly and think. Or, any and all of you could feel free at any time to do the honorable thing.

LEWIS   Which is?

NINA   (*pouring whisky*) Hari-kari.

PERRY   Or whatever. I'm going.

LEWIS   Good-bye.

NINA   Mmm.

                EVELYN walks PERRY to the door.

EVELYN   Perry, I hope you'll be careful.

PERRY   Shouldn't be hard. Don't you run out of here.

EVELYN   I wouldn't. There's nowhere to go but Manhattan, and I'm a stranger there.

                She exhales and looks off. He contemplates her breathtakingly lovely profile.

PERRY   I'll see you soon, Ev— Miss Strange.

EVELYN   Good-bye.

                He goes out and closes the door. There is an
                extended pause in which the others look at one
                another and away.

LEWIS   I wonder if I ought to dress.

NINA   You're at home for the evening. I don't think you're obliged.

LEWIS   Miss Strange, you don't mind?

EVELYN   I have no idea what's appropriate. I wonder though, could I have something to eat? I never did get lunch.

LEWIS   I'm afraid my cupboards are usually bare.

NINA   Make her a rum flip. That has an egg in it.

LEWIS   Miss Strange?

EVELYN   That sounds nice.

LEWIS   (*taking a bottle from the sideboard*) Alright then, I won't be a moment. I...

                He goes into the kitchen.

EVELYN   (*after a pause*) So Mrs. Ferrer, I gather you don't care for opera.

NINA   I can take it or leave it mostly. Some I like, others less so. I do always enjoy Zinka Milanov.

EVELYN   Is that an opera?

NINA   No in fact, it is a person.

EVELYN   Zinka Milanov ... I might have a name like that. I wonder what it would feel like.

NINA   Try it and find out. I expect that's what she did.

EVELYN   Mrs. Ferrer ... Nina. It's kind of you to loan me these clothes, especially under the circumstances.

NINA   Think nothing of it. I've always felt one's appearance should be the last thing to give way.

EVELYN   I suppose what I really meant was that it's kind of you to have anything to do with me at all.

NINA   Well ... I was going to say what choice have I got really, but that's rude. I think it may be generous of you to be speaking to me as well.

EVELYN   Really? Are we friends then?

NINA   I'm going to say not quite yet, though you have probably read my diary.

EVELYN   Yes. I believe I did. And I wrote it as well.

NINA   Accurately too. As one stenographer to another, I must compliment you.

EVELYN   I wonder why I did it?

NINA   I do too. And how and where and when.

EVELYN   Do you think I was going to type it up later?

            NINA gives a little start and opens her eyes wide. LEWIS comes out of the kitchen with a drink.

LEWIS   Here you are Miss Strange. One rum flip.

EVELYN   Thanks. Looks yummy.

            She drains it in two gulps.

            Guess I was hungry.

LEWIS   Another?

EVELYN   (*reeling a little*) Maybe in a while.

            LEWIS notices NINA is breathing through her teeth and clenching her fists.

LEWIS	Nina, what is it? Is your drink empty?
NINA	I supposed I've experienced a moment of clarity and now I'm having to digest another ugly truth.
LEWIS	Can you tell us what it is?
NINA	Miss Strange transcribed my diary so she could type it later. She wrote the first lines in longhand and then switched to shorthand because she found out it was going to be a big job.
EVELYN	That makes sense. And do you think I did type it eventually?
NINA	I'm certain that you did. And I'd bet a fair sum that that's what was in the envelope which was found underneath the dead man in Central Park, who may be a total stranger to me or who may have been my husband.
LEWIS	Please tell us Nina, where did you keep your diary?
NINA	It was in the drawer of my bedside table.
LEWIS	But that's not a secret safe place. Henry could have found it easily.
NINA	Lewis, my bedside table is beside my bed which is in my bedroom. My bedroom. Henry hasn't crossed the threshold of that place for a very long time. It didn't occur to me that he would visit in my absence because he never visited when I was there, and I, perhaps foolishly, assumed that the indifference he felt toward me would also extend to my personal effects.
LEWIS	I think he took your diary and dictated it to Miss Strange and then put it back.
NINA	That's so laborious. She could have typed right from the original.
LEWIS	Unless he didn't want to take it out of the house. Unless he dictated it over the telephone.

EVELYN   Yes! That's it!

                They turn abruptly to EVELYN, who is mildly flustered.

                I mean, it seems likely. It makes sense. I don't know.

                NINA slams down her glass and crosses the room.

                I really wish I could be more help.

NINA   I'm not mad at you, Miss Strange. I'm mad because the police have a copy of my private diary and everyone in New York knows about it. And because my husband went through my personal things. And then he was murdered. Brutally murdered. I could go on and on, but I'm not going to.

LEWIS   Miss Strange, is there anything we can do to jog your memory? What have you tried so far?

EVELYN   Thinking mostly. I've thought and thought till I could almost feel my brain move, but it doesn't seem to help. I looked at everything I passed on the street and I knew what it all was, but I just don't seem to have any associations with anything.

LEWIS   I wonder if hypnosis would help?

EVELYN   You mean where you put me in a trance and ask me questions?

LEWIS   Like that. I didn't mean that I'd do it. I don't think I know how.

NINA   Well, don't look at me. And I think that for hypnosis to take there has to be an atmosphere of trust in the room.

EVELYN   But it's our only constructive idea.

LEWIS   What about if we try to reenact a particular moment from Miss Strange's day yesterday, as far as we can surmise it? Just some particular action or sequence of events that might trigger a memory, or at least help us to make an educated guess about what happened.

EVELYN   Are you saying we'd act it out like a play?

LEWIS   More or less. I'll describe a situation and then you go through the motions in a way that you think makes sense. Nina and I will play the other parts.

NINA   Oh for God's sake, I can't act!

LEWIS   Nina, I think you'll surprise yourself. Now let's just put these chairs together and create a little park bench.

He moves some chairs together and clears any other objects out of the way. NINA applies lipstick, then offers some to EVELYN, who accepts.

I'm just going to dim the lights a little because this probably happened later in the day.

He goes to one side and flicks a light switch.

NINA   What event are we recreating exactly?

LEWIS   This will be Miss Strange's encounter with your husband.

NINA   Ah yes, the heart of the matter. Good thing I've nerves of steel.

LEWIS   We need two coats. One for Miss Strange, and Henry's, which she was wearing earlier.

NINA   She can use my coat. They're both in the bedroom.

She exits into the bedroom.

LEWIS	(*picking up the notepad and taking an envelope from the sideboard*) Now you have the pad with you, and this envelope as well.
EVELYN	Should I have a purse?
LEWIS	Possibly. (*as NINA enters with coats*) Nina, have you got a purse Miss Strange can use?
NINA	Does she need one? She didn't have one with her and there wasn't one found at the scene.
LEWIS	That's right. That's odd, isn't it?
EVELYN	Maybe I'm not carrying one because I'm walking through Central Park at around sundown, and I'm afraid it'll get stolen.
LEWIS	Right, good thinking.
EVELYN	Someone suggested that to me. They gave me that advice.
LEWIS	What? Really?
EVELYN	I think so.
NINA	It might have been Henry. He didn't have his wallet on him either.
LEWIS	Yes! Right! Ladies, we're making progress.
EVELYN	So what's going to happen in this scene?
LEWIS	I want to try a few different approaches. Let's start with you sitting on the bench. You're sitting and waiting, holding the envelope.
EVELYN	(*sitting as described*) Am I afraid?
LEWIS	Not necessarily. Just wait to feel something.
EVELYN	Alright.

> *LEWIS notices NINA sitting in a chair and jiggling slightly.*

LEWIS   Nina, what are you doing?

NINA   I'm on the train from Westchester. I'm going to the opera.

LEWIS   We're doing her day, not yours.

NINA   I thought I was supposed to be in this.

LEWIS   You are. You're going to play Henry.

NINA   Don't you think that'll be perceived as extremely poor taste?

LEWIS   It's ironic and alienating and very modern. Here, put on the coat.

> *NINA scowls at her husband's coat, then puts it on.*

Now, enter cautiously and speak to Miss Strange.

NINA   About?

LEWIS   Business. The reason you're there. The envelope.

NINA   Ah. Yes.

> *She turns and approaches EVELYN.*

Excuse me, Miss Strange? Oh, wait. I can't call her that, can I? How about Miss Smith?

LEWIS   Inspired.

NINA   Miss Smith?

EVELYN   Yes? Mr. Ferrer?

NINA   The same. (*sitting down*) How are you?

EVELYN   Very well. And you?

NINA   Fine thanks. Is that the package containing the typed transcript of my wife's diary which I surreptitiously dictated to you over the phone?

EVELYN   Yes, it is. And this is the shorthand version of same. Shall we make our exchange?

NINA   Certainly. You give me those and I give you ... Oh no. I don't have anything to give you.

EVELYN   Well, I kind of like your coat.

NINA   But it was a gift from my wife. Oh well. (*taking off the coat*) You'll find opera tickets in the pocket, just to make it a bit of a sweeter deal.

EVELYN   Thank you very much, Mr. Ferrer.

  She takes the coat and hands over the envelope and pad, then stands.

  Oh no. I don't remember who I am.

LEWIS   No! Not yet!

EVELYN   What?

NINA   Someone has to shoot me before you lose your memory.

EVELYN   Oh, right.

  She reaches into the pocket of the raincoat and pulls out the gun. She points it at NINA, who screams and ducks behind the chair.

LEWIS   Miss Strange! For God's sake, put that down!

EVELYN   What?

LEWIS   (*taking the gun*) Where did you get this?

EVELYN   I don't know. Who are you?

LEWIS   I'm Lewis. Lewis Hake.

EVELYN   Oh, I see. The scene's over?

LEWIS   Yes, it is. You frightened us. How long have you had
              this gun?

EVELYN   I've always had it, ever since last night.

NINA   Is it loaded?

LEWIS   (*shaking it*) I don't know.

NINA   Wait a minute. I've got something. Miss Strange, sit
              on the bench with me.

EVELYN   Which coat am I wearing?

NINA   Your own. Mine. The dark one. I have Henry's ...
              mine, here beside me. Now Lewis, give me the gun.

LEWIS   But I don't—

NINA   (*snatching the gun*) Just give it to me before I lose my
              train of thought.

              She puts it into the pocket of the coat beside her.

              Now you hand me the packages and we begin.

EVELYN   (*after taking a little breath*) Here you go, Mr. Ferrer.
              All neatly typed, just like you wanted.

NINA   Thank you, Miss Smith. And of course I've something
              for you too.

              She pulls the gun out of the coat pocket.

EVELYN   A gun? But you promised me twenty dollars.

NINA   You don't understand, Miss Smith. You know the
              secret of Evelyn Strange and so you must die.

EVELYN	Oh no! I don't remember who I am!
NINA	No, not yet. I'm still alive!
EVELYN	What?
NINA	(*through clenched teeth*) Fight me.
EVELYN	What?
LEWIS	Fight her ... him. Fight Henry for the gun!
EVELYN	Oh.

They tussle briefly with the gun between them.

| NINA | Bang! |

She falls back, then slumps to the floor.

I'm hit! Oh Nina, what have you cost me?

She expires.

EVELYN	Oh no. I don't know who I am.
NINA	(*sitting up*) How was that? Makes sense to me. Henry could sometimes be a bit of a tightwad.
EVELYN	I don't think it was quite right. No bells went off for me.
LEWIS	Good intensity though, Nina. I believed you.
NINA	Thanks.
LEWIS	But now I'd like to try something. I'm going to be Henry this time.
NINA	Good. I'm tired.
LEWIS	I'll sit on the bench here with the coat lying beside me and Miss Strange, you just approach with the envelope.

EVELYN	Who has the gun?
LEWIS	It doesn't actually matter. Nina, you hang onto it.
EVELYN	Alright, I'm approaching now. Hello? Mr. Ferrer?

He stares ahead.

Mr. Ferrer? It's me, Miss Smith, the dicta-typist. I've got your manuscript here, sir.

He doesn't respond. She looks perplexed.

NINA	Give him a poke.
EVELYN	Oh. (*poking him*) Poke.

He slumps over, as though dead.

Mr. Ferrer, what 's wrong?

LEWIS	(*whispering*) I'm dead. I'm dead already. Someone shot me.

EVELYN bursts out laughing. LEWIS sits up.

What's so funny?

EVELYN	Well you were lying there dead and I just asked you what was wrong. Don't you think that's funny? You probably had a hole in your head and everything.
LEWIS	(*laughing a little*) That's true.
EVELYN	(*still laughing*) And so I ask you "What's wrong?" and you say "I'm dead. Someone shot me in the head."

EVELYN and LEWIS laugh and laugh.

NINA	Alright, that's enough! This is it. This is exactly what happened. You two sit on the bench. The coat is there beside Henry. Miss Smith has the envelope and you make the exchange, which is for twenty dollars.

LEWIS   Alright.

NINA withdraws to one side.

LEWIS   Have you got the package, Miss Smith?

EVELYN   Yes, here it is.

LEWIS   Good. And here's your twenty dollars.

He reaches into the coat pocket and is a little surprised to find a twenty dollar bill. He hands it to EVELYN.

EVELYN   Thank you very much.

LEWIS   And thank you.

NINA runs forward, brandishing the gun.

NINA   Aha!! Here you are, Henry Ferrer! I've caught you red-handed and I don't mean with the girl. How dare you steal my diary! You've no business knowing my most private thoughts. They have no place in your brain and that's why I'm going to put a hole in your head! Blam! Blam-blam-blam!! Ah hahahahaha!!!

EVELYN and LEWIS stare at NINA.

Oh. I don't come out of this looking too good, do I? And, I suppose this gun has my fingerprints all over it now.

EVELYN   That didn't really stir anything up for me. I'd say you're off the hook.

NINA   (*dropping the gun on the bench beside LEWIS*) Good. I don't think I ought to play anymore.

EVELYN   Maybe this isn't going to work. I don't want to waste everyone's time just on account of my mind.

LEWIS   We're just going too fast. If we can just piece our way through this as carefully as possible.

> *Contemplating intently, he leans forward, placing his elbows on his knees and his head in his hands.*

EVELYN   Lewis!

LEWIS   What?

EVELYN   The way you're sitting... That's right. Just stay like that.

LEWIS   Like this?

EVELYN   Yes.

> *She stares at him for some time, then slowly backs away. She stands and stares at him for another moment before coming forward and initiating a very slow, quiet conversation.*

EVELYN   Hello? Excuse me ... Mr. Ferrer?

LEWIS   (*looking up slowly*) Yes. You must be ...

EVELYN   Yes, I have your manuscript here.

LEWIS   Good. Thank you for coming. Will you sit down?

EVELYN   Just for a minute. It's getting darker, and I don't want to stay too long in the park.

LEWIS   Of course. Maybe I shouldn't have asked you to come here. I just wanted to do this somewhere out of the way because—

EVELYN   You don't have to explain. It's not my business.

LEWIS   Thank you.

EVELYN   (*giving him the manuscript*) Well, here you go.

LEWIS   Thank you. And here's your fee. I hope twenty dollars is alright.

EVELYN   Twenty dollars is a lot. It's more than my whole rent.

LEWIS   Well, I know it must have been unpleasant for you to
       type something like this.

EVELYN   Oh no, not at all. There are racy bits but I wouldn't
       dream of judging the person who wrote them. That
       woman. Evelyn Strange ... She was just so happy.
       She says she lived her life with more sense than
       passion, and I think everybody does that, but the thing
       of it is that that doesn't make any sense. It doesn't
       make sense if it's not what you want. So, my face
       may have turned red a little in some of these passages,
       and I'd be embarrassed if I ever had to talk about that
       sort of thing myself, but I'm glad somebody did it. I'm
       glad somebody got to do what they wanted, and I think
       people might be glad to know that it happened. I think
       it might cheer you up a bit. It's not my place to
       remark on it, but you did look a little down, when I
       first saw you and—

LEWIS   You forget. I've already read it.

EVELYN   Of course, that's right. Well maybe you won't ... This
       really isn't my business at all. I'd better be going.

       She gets up.

       Oh, did you want this notepad? It's just my shorthand
       copy that I took off the phone.

LEWIS   No thanks. Just throw it away.

EVELYN   Alright. Well, thanks for the job. You have my
       number, if you need anything else typed.

LEWIS   Yes. Thank you.

EVELYN   Good-bye.

LEWIS   Good-bye.

       *She turns and walks away behind him. She stands
       still for a moment. LEWIS turns a little to see her.*

      So, after that—

The introduction to Act Two of "Siegfried" begins to play quietly, underscoring what follows

EVELYN   (*slowly and intently*) I'm walking away ... I'm walking through the park... I want to get back to the main path... I'm walking through the park and I'm starting to hear sounds.

> *There is a quiet knock at the door. EVELYN turns away and covers her face with her hands. NINA opens the door and admits PERRY.*

PERRY   What's happening? Where are the lights?

NINA   Shh!

> *She closes the door and pulls PERRY into a corner.*

EVELYN   I have to get back to the path, but I have to go through too many trees. I have twenty dollars in my coat and that's making me a little nervous. I really don't think I want to go all this way by myself. I don't think I can. I know it isn't far, but it's not safe and I'm sure if I go back and ask Mr. Ferrer, he'd...

> *She turns and walks up behind LEWIS.*

Mr. Ferrer, I know you'll think me a bit silly, but suddenly I'm a bit frightened and-

> *LEWIS has been leaning forward as before, but turned to one side. As she speaks, he turns toward her, with the gun raised to his head. Their eyes meet for a split second. EVELYN gasps.*

LEWIS   Bang.

> *A live gunshot is heard. EVELYN screams and the scene turns completely red. The music continues to play, now at a much higher level.*

NINA   NO!!

> *PERRY holds NINA tightly. NINA screams again
> as LEWIS falls against her. She catches him and
> quickly pushes him back onto the bench where he
> lays on top of the envelope. EVELYN backs away
> a little, whimpering and crying and looks at
> herself in horror, as though discovering
> bloodstains on her coat. She takes it off and drops
> it to the ground.*
>
> *After discarding her coat, EVELYN picks up the
> raincoat from the bench and puts it on. She
> notices her notebook on the ground and bends
> down to pick it up. As she does so, she sees the
> gun where LEWIS has let it fall. She picks up
> both and puts them in her coat pocket, then picks
> up her coat and drapes it over LEWIS. She backs
> away, then turns and stands in utter confusion.
> She takes steps in a few different directions, then
> runs into a corner.*

PERRY   (*approaching her*) Evelyn ... Miss Strange ...

> *He touches her arm. She looks at him with an
> expression of stark terror and hurtles across the
> room where she collapses sobbing in another
> corner. LEWIS uncovers himself and sits up.
> NINA flings herself down beside him and sobs
> violently onto his chest. The music stops.*

NINA   He killed himself! He killed himself because of us.
Lewis! My poor Henry! It shouldn't have happened
like that! It didn't have to end so badly!

LEWIS   Nina, please. Don't—

NINA   And I had to watch it happen! I had to sit here and
watch him blow his brains out and know it was all my
fault.

LEWIS   You can't say that. Just because—

NINA   It's not just our affair. I may never have loved my
husband the way I wanted to love someone but there
was a time when I respected him and enjoyed his

company. And then ... And then he named his
business Ferrer and Sons and it was all over. I couldn't
live with that pressure, those expectations ... So I
turned away from him. Not forcefully, not with any
kind of final statement. I just withdrew, and before
long it seemed understood that there were no bonds of
intimacy between us. I hoped... I thought it must not
have mattered to him. I was so wrong!

She continues to sob in LEWIS' arms.

PERRY   (*approaching*) Nina... Lewis ... I know that this may
not be the moment for it, but I have to show you
something ... something I found in Henry's office.

NINA groans slightly and looks up.

LEWIS   What is it?

PERRY   (*taking a black book from his jacket pocket*) It's
Henry's datebook, the one he kept on his desk. I
looked at the entries for yesterday and there's really
nothing of interest. Just some morning meetings and
the opera at seven. Nothing about anything else after
work.

LEWIS   But we know now. We know what happened at that
time.

PERRY   That's true, and the daily calendar isn't what's of
interest here. All sorts of meetings and social
engagements but none that offer any sort of clues
about anything out of the ordinary. But when you turn
to this appendix at the back, you find this other set of
schedules. You see ... month by month, all the dates
projected for final drafts, proofing, books going to
press, shipping dates, launches ... And here, pencilled
at the bottom of every list, a new book scheduled for
release on the seventh of November.

LEWIS   (*looking at the book*) Diary E.S.. Diary E.S. Diary
E.S. You mean to say...

NINA   (*very slowly*) He was going to publish THE DIARY OF EVELYN STRANGE on the seventh of November. That would have been our tenth wedding anniversary.

LEWIS   Oh Nina.

> *NINA is trembling. She stands up, her face contorting.*

NINA   THAT BASTARD GOT WHAT HE DESERVED!! How could he do that to me? How could he set me up for that kind of public humiliation?

PERRY   It may be that he didn't intend to put your name on it.

NINA   But he would know and I would know and so he would have crushed me. It can't happen! It mustn't happen!

LEWIS   Nina, it's not going to. Henry is dead. It was up to him to complete this terrible project and he chose not to. That should be painfully clear.

NINA   But why? Why would he go so far with this and then just give up?

LEWIS   Maybe it was what the stenographer said..."That woman. Evelyn Strange ... She was just so happy."

NINA   But he must have hated that.

LEWIS   Not if he realized he loved ... her.

NINA   Her?

LEWIS   Not if he realized that he too loved Evelyn Strange.

> *NINA emits a sharp involuntary cry and crosses away. She stands to one side, her back to the room.*

PERRY   I don't understand why he had the gun. He must have been considering killing himself all along.

LEWIS	Yes, that's true. Unless he was planning something worse. Something ... messy.
PERRY	Like what?
LEWIS	(*after a little pause*) Let's not speculate, since it didn't happen. (*looking at EVELYN*) What about her? Did you find out anything about her?
PERRY	I may have.
NINA	(*turning abruptly*) Lewis, I want to go to the police.
LEWIS	You do?
NINA	It's the only way out of this. We've known it all along, though none of us has had the courage to say so.

PERRY bites his lip.

LEWIS	What will you tell them?
NINA	That my husband is missing. That the dead man has my diary. I suppose I'll have to see the body.
LEWIS	But what if they suspect you?
NINA	What if they do? I'm not guilty.
LEWIS	Of course.

He offers her the dark overcoat.

NINA	I can't wear that. The blood...
LEWIS	But it isn't really—
NINA	Lewis, let's just go.
LEWIS	Alright.
PERRY	You're not dressed, Lewis.

LEWIS   (*stopping in his tracks*) Oh. Yes. Nina. I—

NINA   Right now I'm very calm and very well focussed. But I could lash out at any moment and drag you all into my personal lake of fire. Does anyone want that to happen? Lewis?

LEWIS   No.

NINA   Then take me to the police. NOW!!

LEWIS   Fine.

PERRY   The precinct is just around the corner.

LEWIS   Yes. I know. That makes it better.

     He opens the door for NINA.

     But what about her. Miss Strange? Shouldn't she come along? To explain—

NINA   I am Evelyn Strange and that should be enough for anyone.

     She goes out.

PERRY   We'll be along as soon as we can.

LEWIS   Thanks.

     He tightens the belt on his dressing gown and goes out, shutting the door behind him. PERRY hurries over to EVELYN, who is still crouching in a corner.

PERRY   Evel— Miss Stran— Are you alright?

EVELYN   (*crawling away from him*) I've got to get somewhere. I've got to get downtown, I think ... downtown. I have a ticket. I have a ticket for the Metropolitan Opera. That must be where I should be. I have to go!

PERRY   No, wait. That's past now. You've been there.

EVELYN   No. I'm going there.

PERRY   You've remembered what happened in the park. Do
         you know who you are now? Do you remember your
         name?

EVELYN   (*struggling*) Leave me alone! I have to go down Park
         Avenue! I have to go to "Siegfried".

PERRY   No, listen to me! You've already seen it. We saw it
         together. You sat in a box! You came to my office.
         You met Lewis Hake and Nina Ferrer. Well maybe
         you don't want to remember them, but there was The
         Automat and the Livonia Hotel. But the opera ... just
         try to remember the opera. You enjoyed "Siegfried".
         You wanted to be Brunhilde. Remember them? And
         Fafner? You must remember Fafner!

         *EVELYN is on the ground facing away from
         PERRY, practically lying down. She holds very
         still.*

EVELYN   Faf ... ner ... Fafner was the dragon...

PERRY   Yes. Yes, he was.

EVELYN   Fafner was the dragon Brunhilde ... Perry ... Perry
         Spangler.

PERRY   Yes, yes, that's me. Now you're getting it. Do you
         remember what you saw yesterday in Central Park?

EVELYN   I saw. I saw a man take his own life.

PERRY   And before that ... What did you do?

EVELYN   I typed. I typed all day.

PERRY   Where did you do it? Where did you type?

EVELYN   At home. At my home. I used to type in an office, but
         I don't now ... I lost my job.

> *They are still on the floor. She is looking down and away from him.*

PERRY You lost your job and so you type at home. How does that work?

EVELYN I advertise. I put an ad in the paper.

PERRY In *The Daily News*. You put an ad (*taking a clipping from his pocket*) in *The Daily News* and my boss saw it and circled it.

> *He puts the clipping in front of her.*

EVELYN "Will type anything fast. Call Miss Tremayne. 237-6538." That's it. That's my ad.

PERRY You're Miss Tremayne.

EVELYN (*collapsing face down*) I'm Miss Tremayne! I know it—

PERRY (*kneeling over her*) Miss Tremayne. I'm Mr. Spangler.

EVELYN What?

PERRY I'm introducing myself. (*speaking very deliberately*) I'm Mr. Spangler and I'm very pleased to meet you, Miss Tremayne.

EVELYN (*also deliberately and slowly*) I'm pleased to meet you also, Mr. Spangler.

PERRY I'd be delighted if you'd call me Perry.

EVELYN Perry? Then you must call me ... you must call me ... Sheila.

PERRY Sheila? Sheila Tremayne?

> *There is a long pause, slowly she turns over and raises herself into his embrace as radiant orchestral strains of Brunhilde's Awakening from "Siegfried" are heard.*

EVELYN Oh Perry Spangler, I know you as Brunhilde knew Siegfried and as she knew herself I know myself too.

PERRY Sheila. Sheila Tremayne.

EVELYN That's my name. Ask me again and I'll tell ya the same. (*gasping*) Oh no!

PERRY What is it?

EVELYN I broke up with my fiancé.

PERRY When?

EVELYN Two weeks ago. Just before I lost my job.

> *She sniffles a little.*

PERRY Sheila, I think I'm here to tell you that none of that matters now.

EVELYN It doesn't? Why not?

PERRY Well to put it squarely, because you've met me. You met me and we went on a date. We went to the opera and The Automat and we had a terrific time. Okay, it was a little awkward occasionally, but what first date isn't? I'd like to take you out again if I may.

EVELYN Perry, I think that would be fine. How about tonight? Do you have plans?

PERRY I thought we might scoot by the police station and give a statement, but after that we can do whatever you like. (*getting out his wallet and looking in it*) Or can we?

EVELYN (*checking the pocket of the dark overcoat*) Here, I think I have ... twenty dollars. And there should be another twenty in the coat that was recovered in the park. They'll have to give that back to me. I earned it.

PERRY You certainly did.

EVELYN   So, can we go to the opera again tonight?

PERRY   I suppose so. I don't know what's playing, but it's
          bound to be shorter.

EVELYN   I like the long ones. I can lose myself in them.

PERRY   Maybe we should just go dancing.

EVELYN   Oh that'd be fine too. But Perry...

PERRY   Yes?

EVELYN   Earlier today, you kissed me, didn't you?

PERRY   I'll admit I did. I wanted to apologize but you said I
          didn't have to while you were missing your identity.
          Now that you've found it I guess it falls to me to—

EVELYN   No. Wait. The problem is I don't really remember that
          kiss vividly enough to say whether it merits an
          apology.

PERRY   Should we just drop it then?

EVELYN   That's not quite what I was thinking.

PERRY   I see. Well then...

          *Siegfried and Brunhilde are heard rejoicing in
          song. Evelyn and Perry approach one another and
          lock lips on the final triumphant high 'C'.*

          They break apart.

EVELYN   Perry Spangler, bring me before the law!

PERRY   Sheila Tremayne, I shall!

Accompanied by the raucous concluding bars of "Siegfried", they gather up the coats, the gun and the notebook and exit triumphantly, closing the door behind them.

The End.